Dunnville Ontario Book 1 in Colour Photos, Saving Our History One Photo at a Time

Photography
by Barbara Raué
©2021

Series Name: Cruising Ontario

Book 214: Dunnville Book 1

Cover photo: 431 Queen Street, Page 58

©All the photos in this book have been taken with my cameras. I own the rights to them.

Series Name: Cruising Ontario Saving Our History One Photo at a Time in colour photos

Books Available in Alphabetical Order:
Aberfoyle, Acton, Ajax, Alton, Amherstburg, Ancaster, Arthur, Auburn, Aylmer, Ayr, Beaver Valley, Belgrave, Belleville, Bloomingdale, Blyth, Brantford, Brockville, Burford, Burlington, Caledon, Caledonia, Cambridge, Carlow, Chatsworth, Clifford, Collingwood, Conestogo, Delhi, Dorchester to Aylmer, Drayton, Drumbo, Dundas, Dunlop, Eden Mills, Elmira, Elora, Erin, Essex, Fergus, Goderich, Grimsby, Guelph, Hagersville, Hamilton, Hanover, Harriston, Hespeler, Jarvis, Kingston, Kingsville, Kitchener, Lake Superior, Lincoln, Linwood, Listowel, London, Lucknow, Merrickville, Mono, Mount Forest, Mount Pleasant, Neustadt, New Hamburg, Newboro, Newport, Niagara-on-the-Lake, Niagara Falls, North Bay, Oakville, Onondaga, Orangeville, Orillia, Oshawa, Owen Sound, Palmerston, Paris, Pelham, Perth, Peterborough, Petrolia, Pickering, Port Colborne, Port Elgin, Portland, Preston, Rockwood, Sarnia, Sault Ste. Marie, Seaforth, Sheffield, Shelburne, Simcoe, Smiths Falls, Smithville, Southampton, St. Catharines, St. George, St. Jacobs, St. Marys, St. Thomas, Stoney Creek, Stratford, Thamesford, Thunder Bay, Tillsonburg, Toronto, Waterdown, Waterford, Waterloo, Welland, Wellesley, West Flamborough, Westport, Whitby, Windsor, Wingham, Woodstock

Book 210: North Bay
Book 211: Fort Erie
Book 212-215: Haldimand
    County

Table of Contents

Broad Street West	Page 5
Broad Street East	Page 19
Niagara Street	Page 31
Tamarac Street	Page 35
Lock Street	Page 36
Queen Street	Page 54
Helena Street	Page 59
Cedar Street	Page 61
Church Street	Page 61
Chestnut Street	Page 62
North Shore Drive	Page 66

Dunnville is a community near the mouth of Grand River in Haldimand County, and is only a few kilometers from Lake Erie. Dunnville was one of the early thriving centers of Upper Canada and Ontario. Following the American Revolution, a six mile strip of land on both sides of the Grand River from its mouth to its sources was opened up to settlement by displaced members of the Six Nations Confederacy. The land was granted to the Iroquois tribes by the British to compensate the Confederacy for land lost in the United States during the revolution.

The British originally intended the land to remain in the hands of the Indians, but Mohawk Chief Joseph Brant wanted to open it up to settlement in order to create a source of revenue. Brant persuaded the Six Nations to surrender large blocks of land. Many of the early European arrivals were United Empire Loyalists.

By 1825, twenty-five people lived around Dunnville with a grist mill, a saw mill, and a distillery owned by Squire Anthony who was perhaps the first settler in the area. William Hamilton Merritt is called the Father of Canadian Transportation. With his vision and energy the Feeder Canal connected Dunnville to the rest of the Welland Canal which flowed from Port Dalhousie on Lake Ontario to Welland. Large amounts of timber were shipped by scows from the Grand River to Buffalo and other markets for use as fuel for the new and growing railroads. The initial Dunnville Dam was finished in 1829, in time for the opening of the Welland Canal in November of that year. The project brought laborers to the area, creating a need for farm produce and housing.The damming of the river provided a reliable source of power which supported mills and businesses including a tannery and a cloth factory. Dunnville was also served by the Buffalo, Brantford and Goderich Railway and was an important port which warranted its own government customs office.

By 1907, Dunnville had four large textile mills. Textiles continued to fuel the town's development for many years.

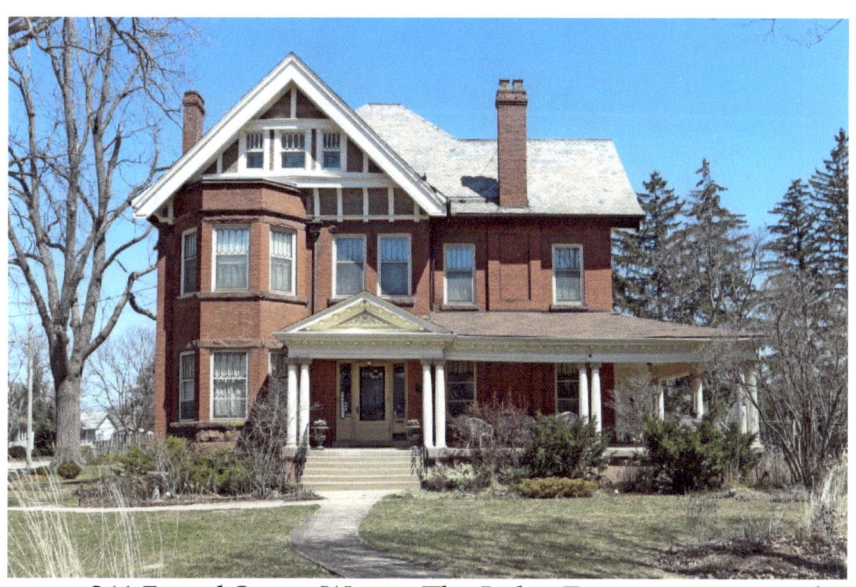

241 Broad Street West – The Lalor Estate is a two-and-a-half-storey residence with a four-gable roof and a wraparound veranda with fluted columns. This Edwardian structure was built in 1905. Its builder was Francis Ramsey Lalor, a prominent Dunnville businessman, politician, philanthropist, and entrepreneur. His business interests included two dry goods stores, a grocery store, an apple evaporator, natural gas wells, the F.R. Lalor Canning Factories, the F.R. Lalor Ashes Company, and the Monarch Knitting Mills.

The exterior walls are red brick. There is a two-storey bay window, Tudor-style timbering in the gable, a pediment above the entrance with a decorative tympanum, and sidelights beside the front door.

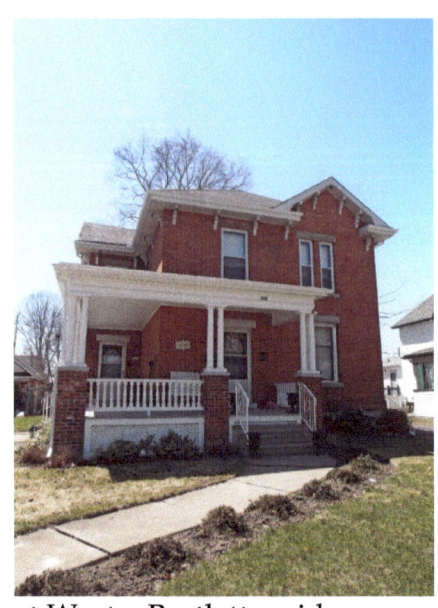

210 Broad Street West – Bartlett residence – c. 1901 - hipped roof, cornice brackets, wraparound veranda

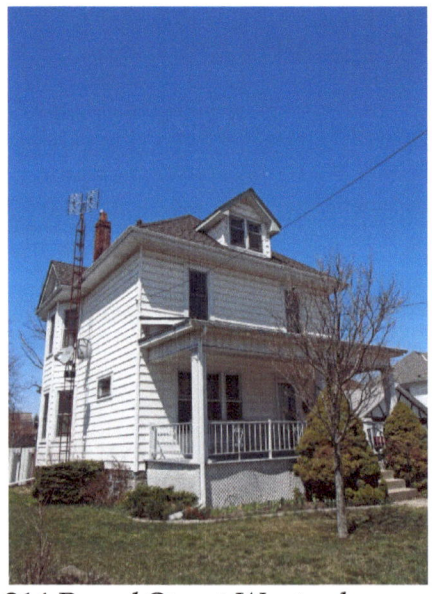

214 Broad Street West - dormer

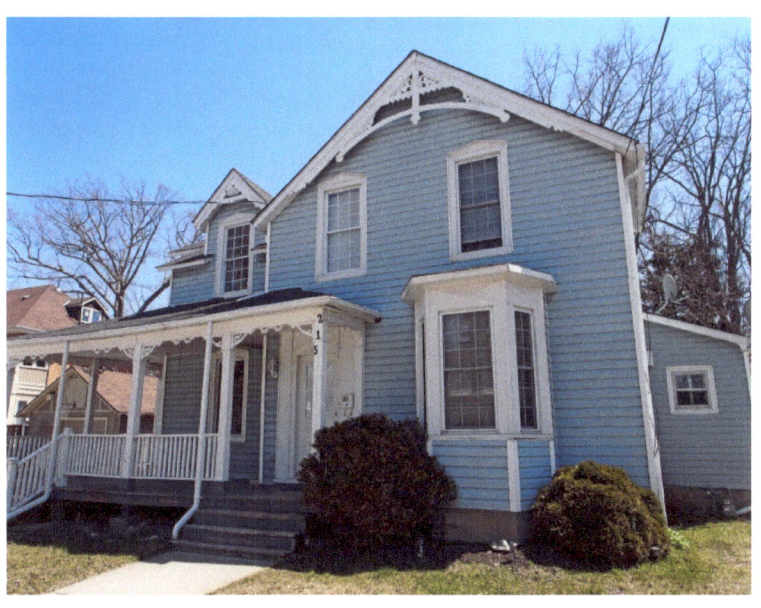

#215-217 – verge board trim on gables, bay window, second floor side balcony

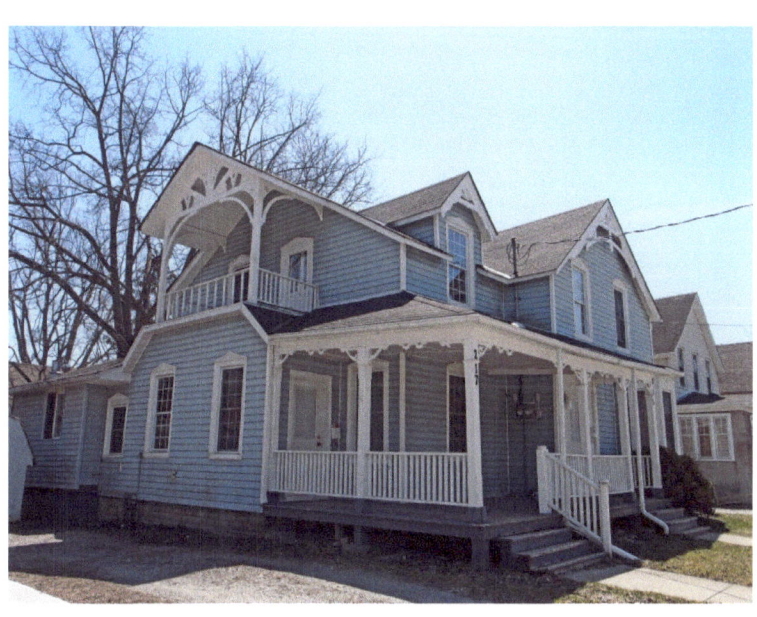

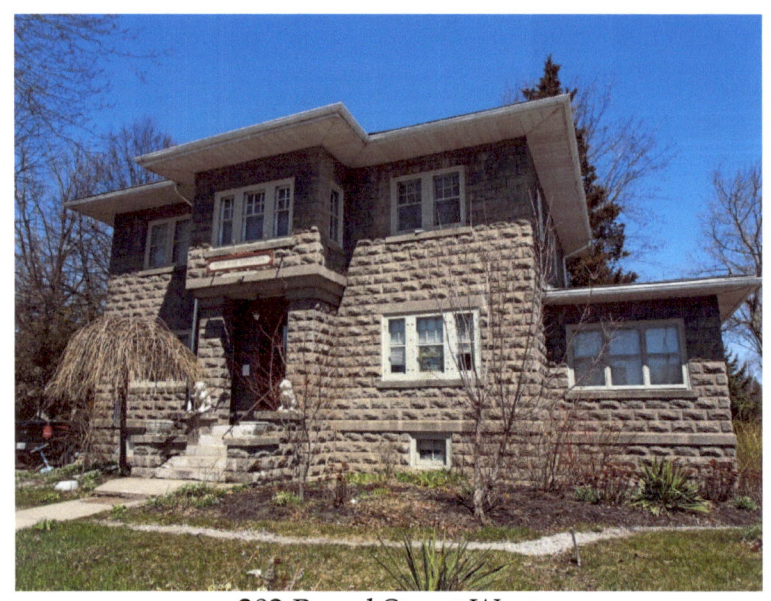

203 Broad Street West

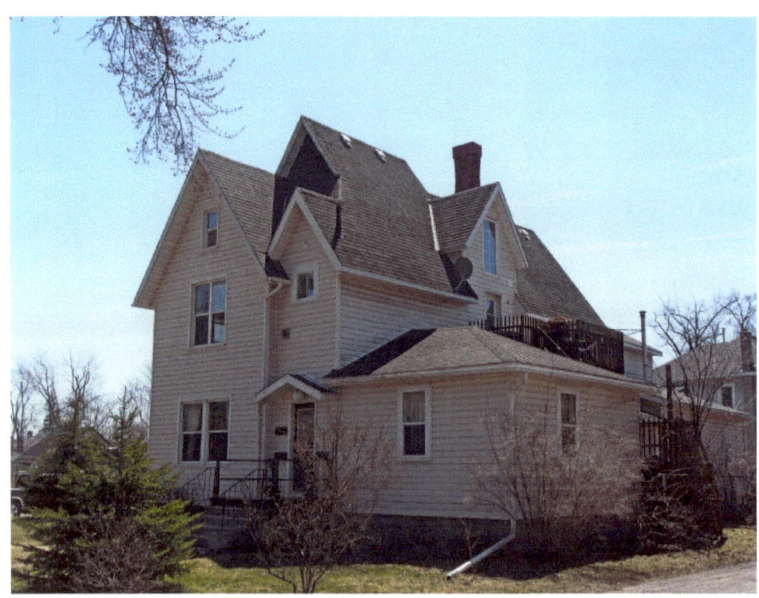

Broad Street West

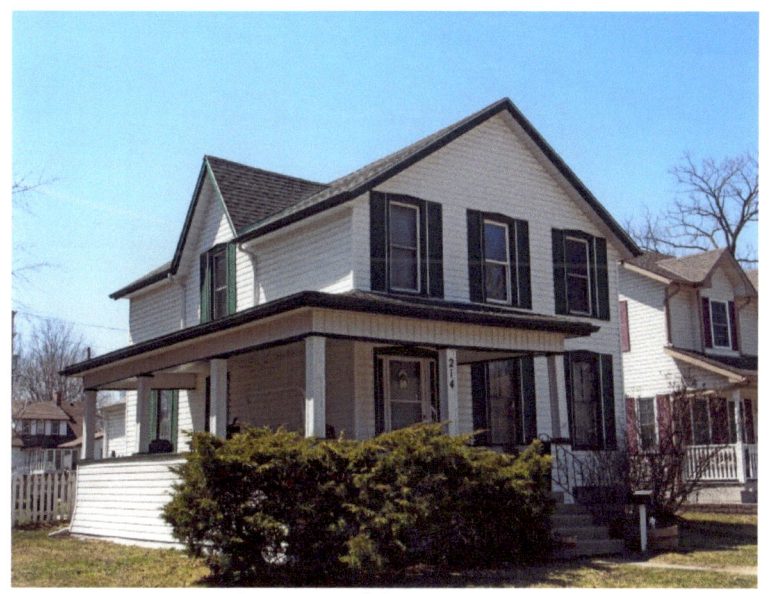

214 Broad Street West

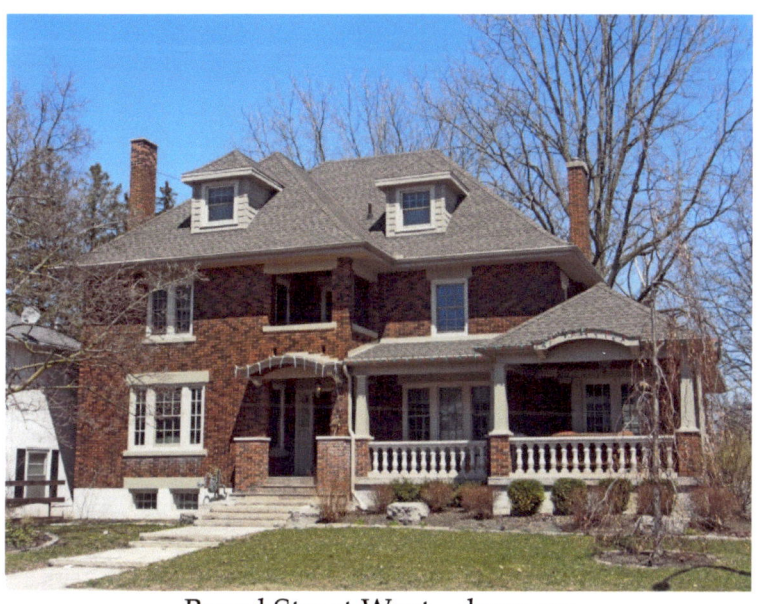

Broad Street West - dormers

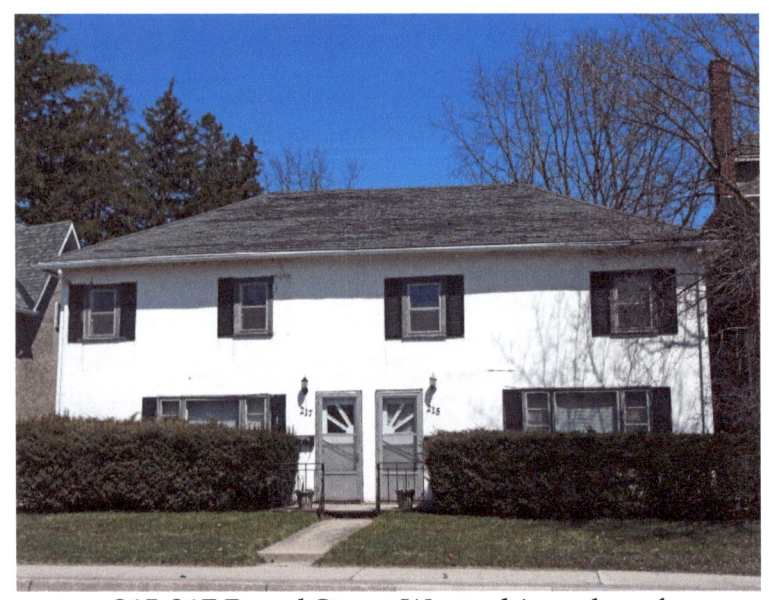

215-217 Broad Street West – hipped roof

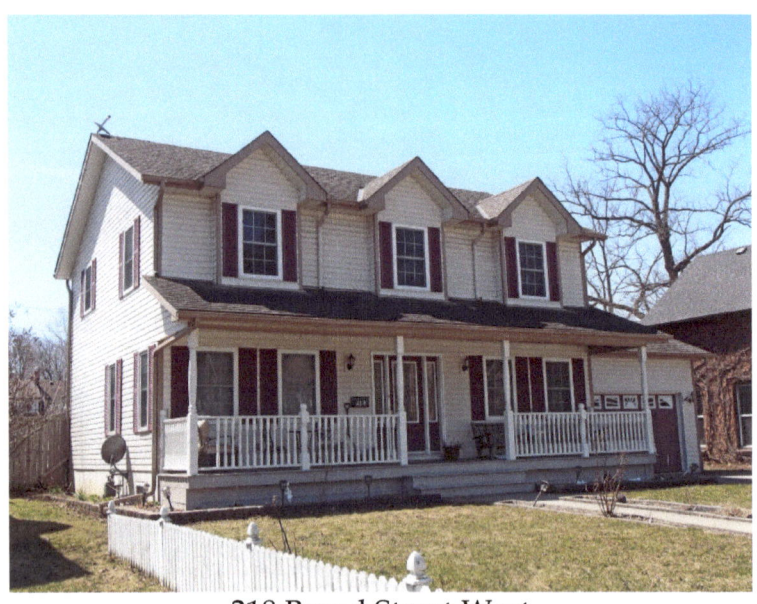

218 Broad Street West

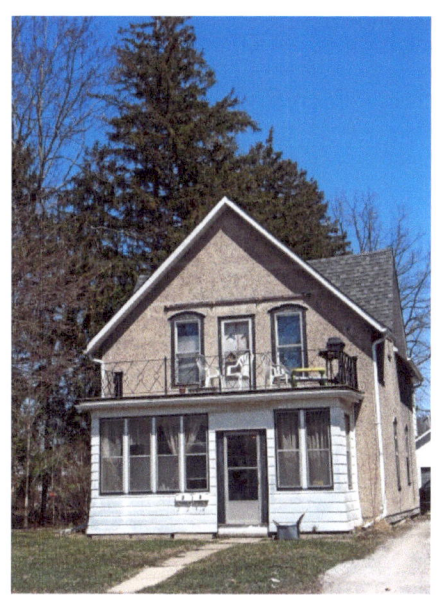

Broad Street West

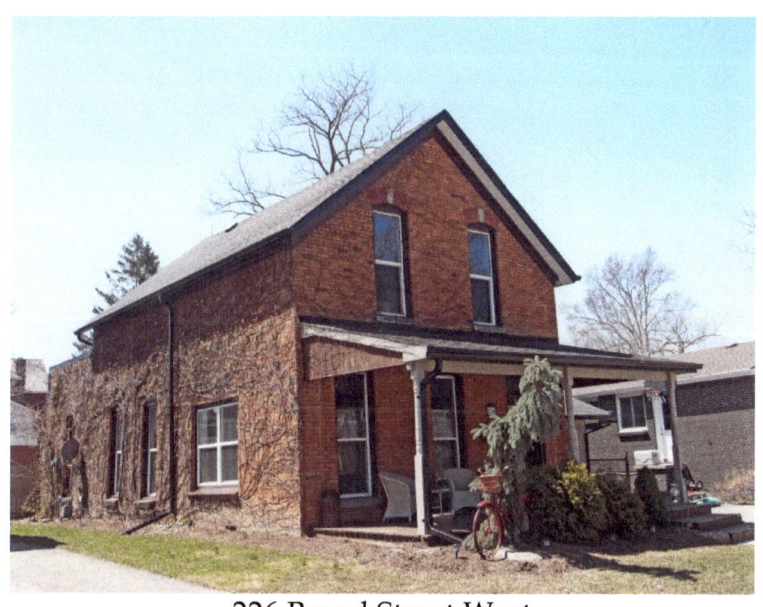

226 Broad Street West

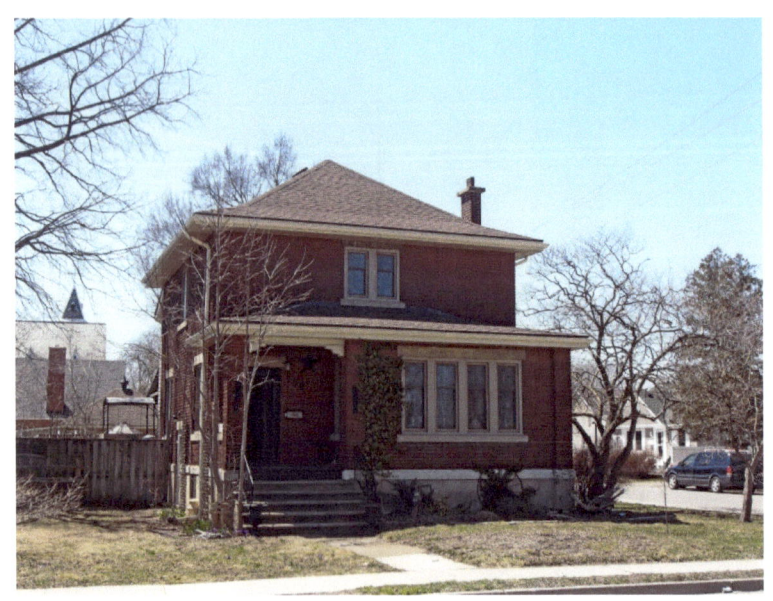

250 Broad Street West

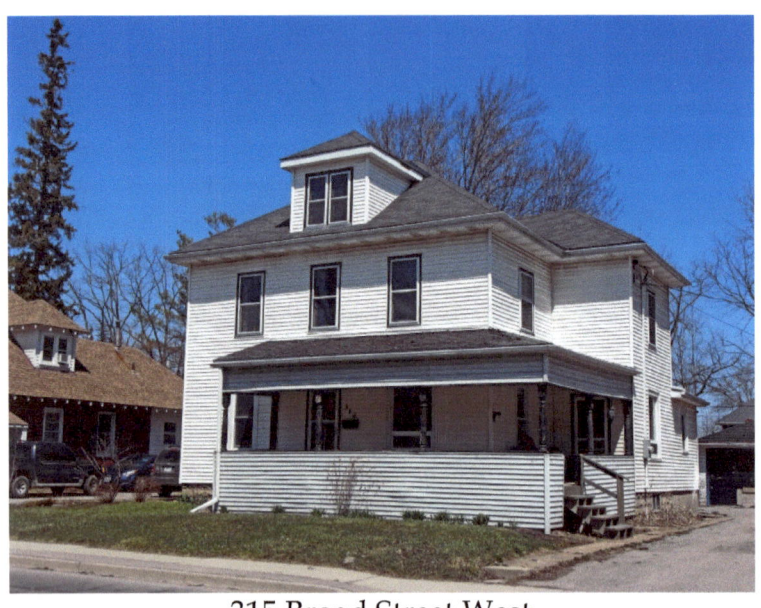

315 Broad Street West

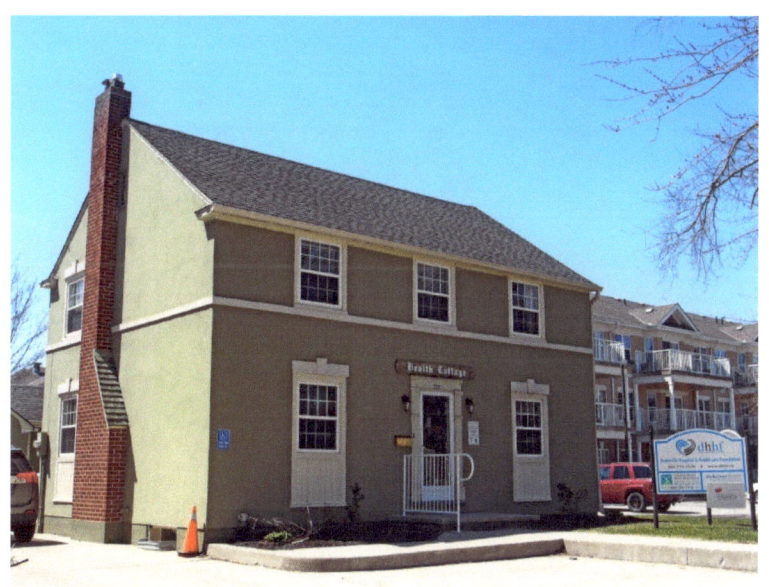

322 Broad Street West

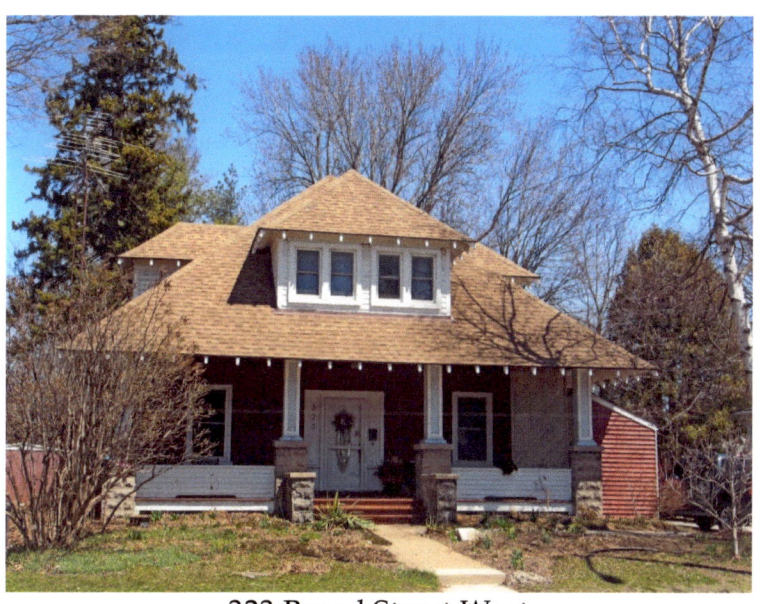

323 Broad Street West

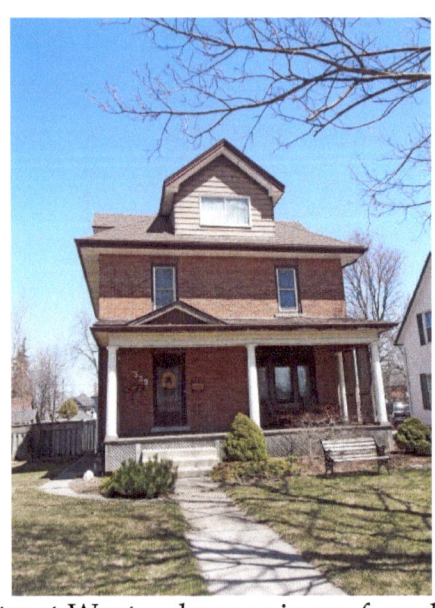

329 Broad Street West – dormer in roof, pediment above entrance

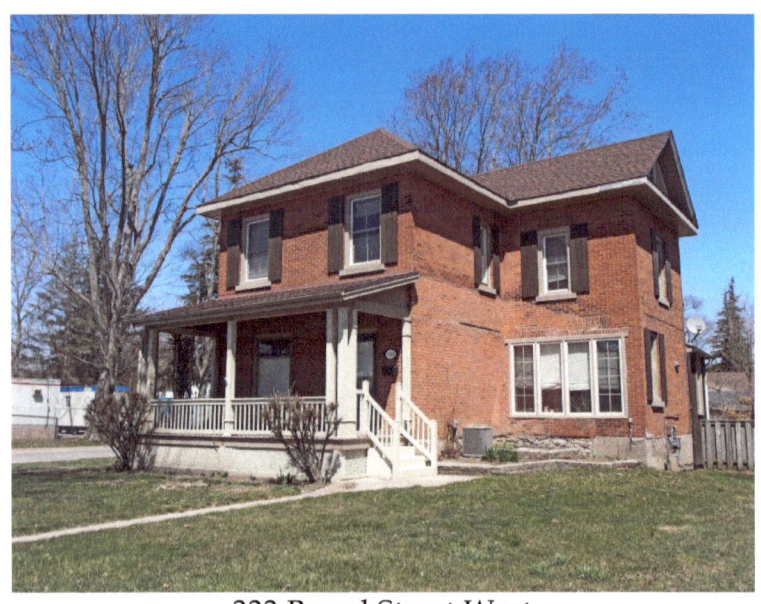

333 Broad Street West

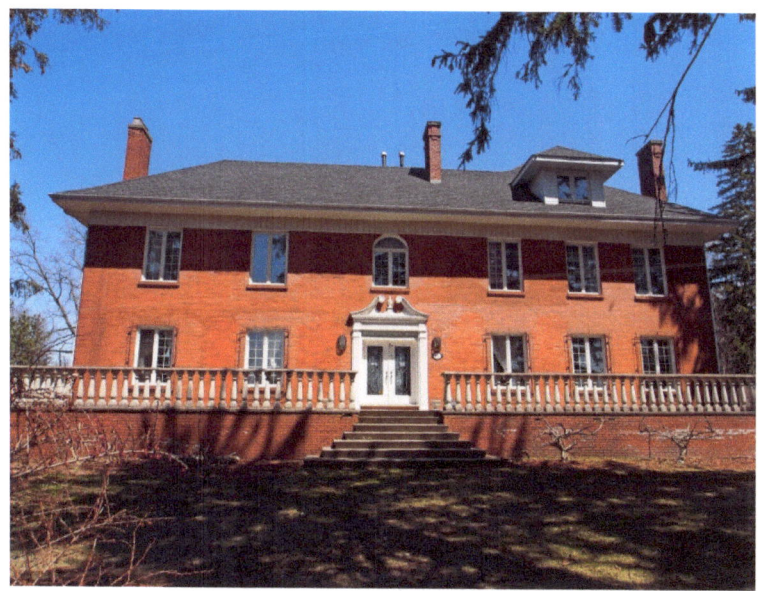

417 Broad Street West – Georgian style, broken pediment above entrance, multi-paned windows

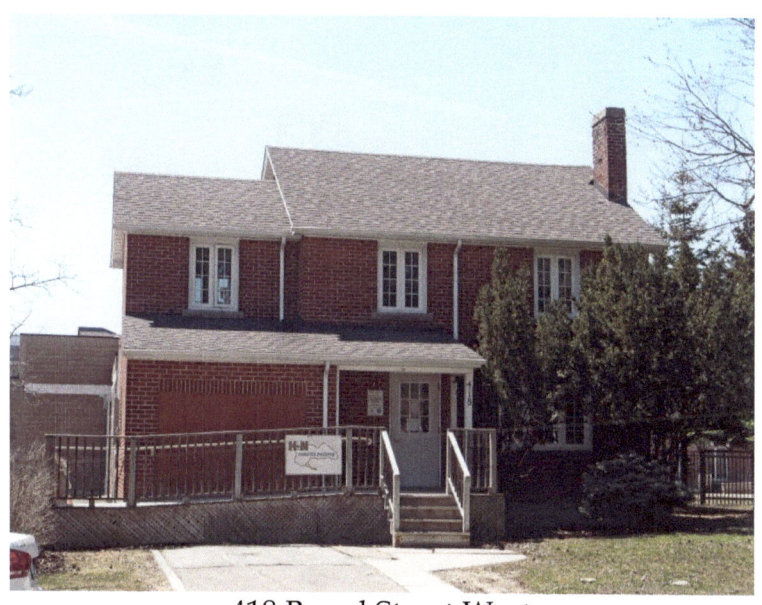

418 Broad Street West

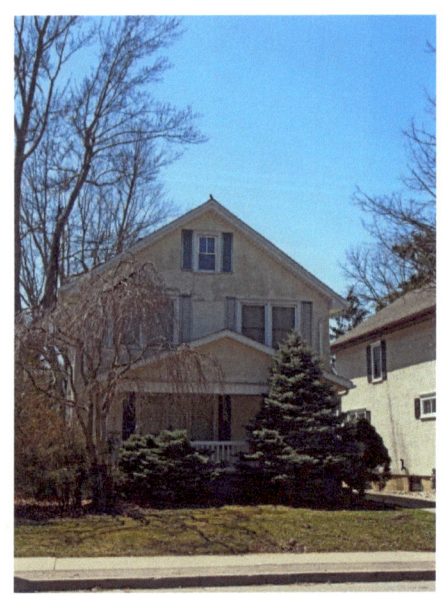

432 Broad Street West

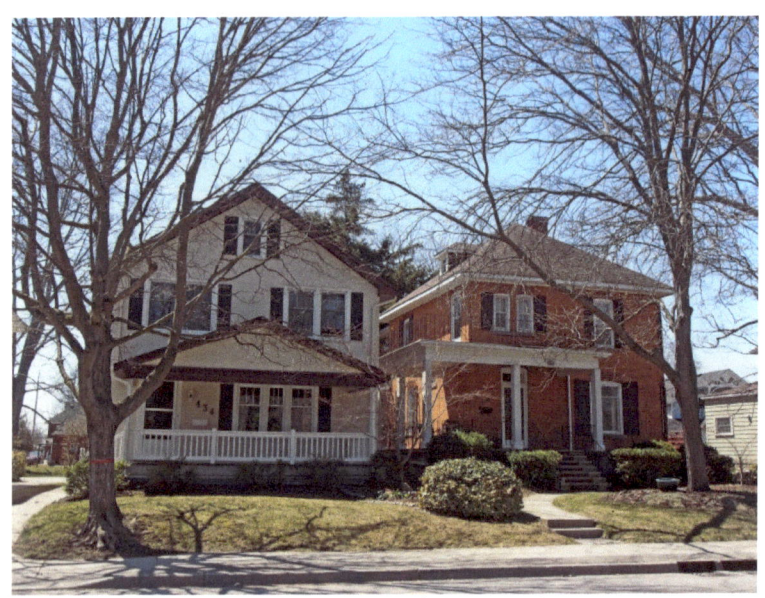

434 and 438 Broad Street West

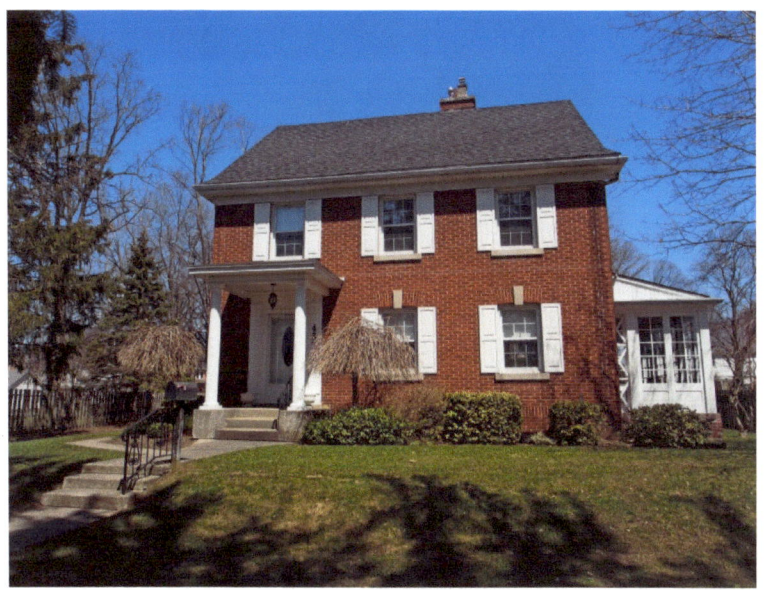

433 Broad Street West

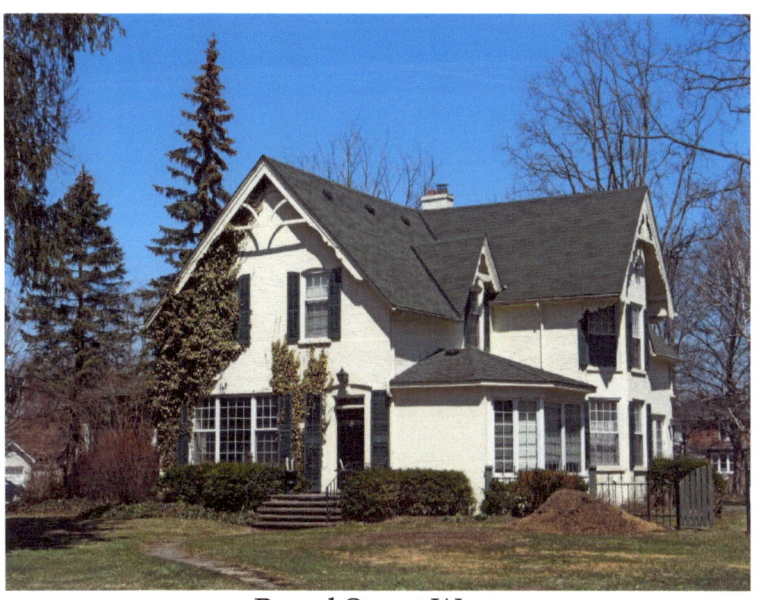

Broad Street West

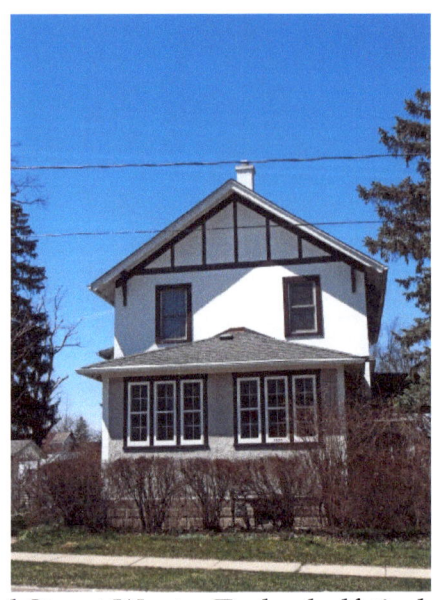

Broad Street West – Tudor half-timbering

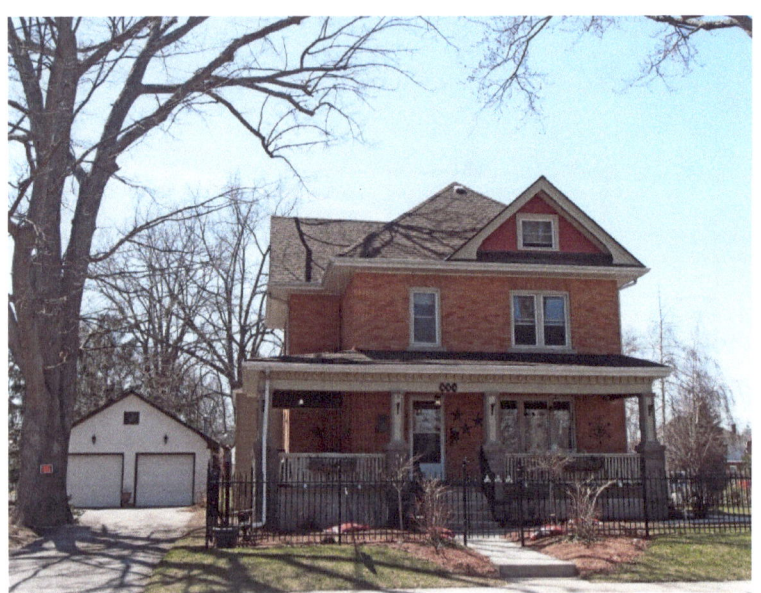

444 Broad Street West

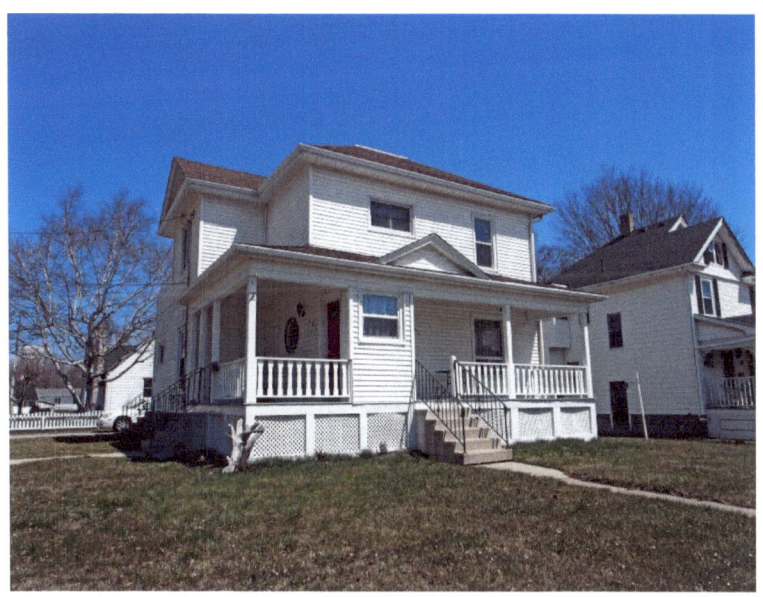

601 Broad Street East

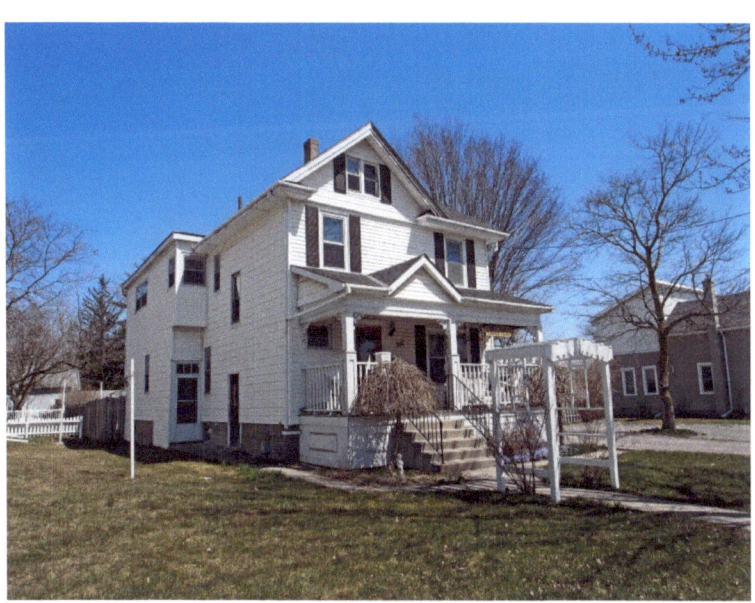

607 Broad Street East

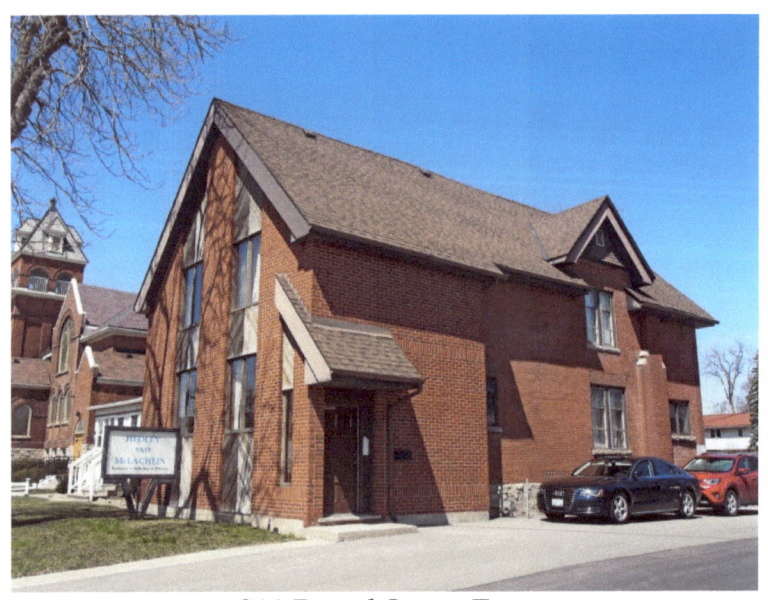

311 Broad Street East

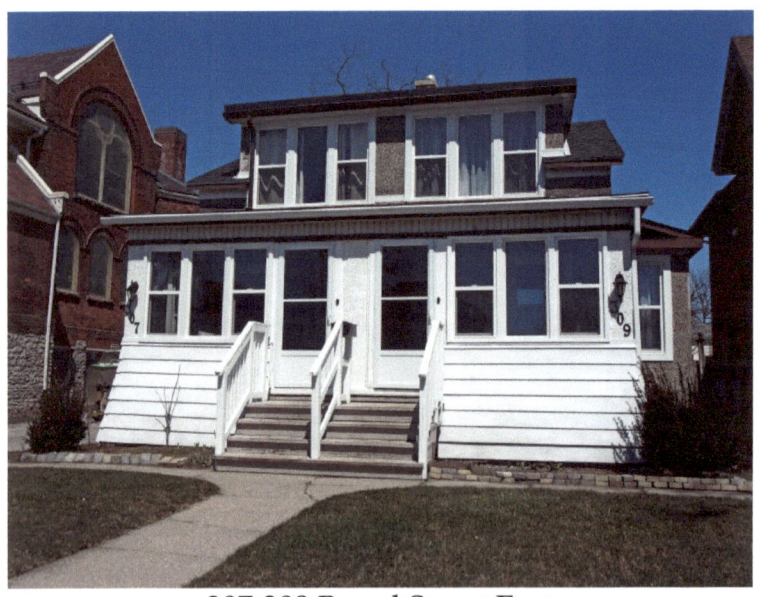

307-309 Broad Street East

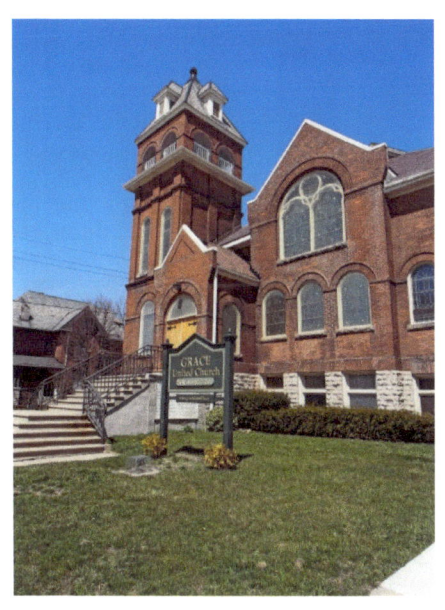

301 Broad Street East

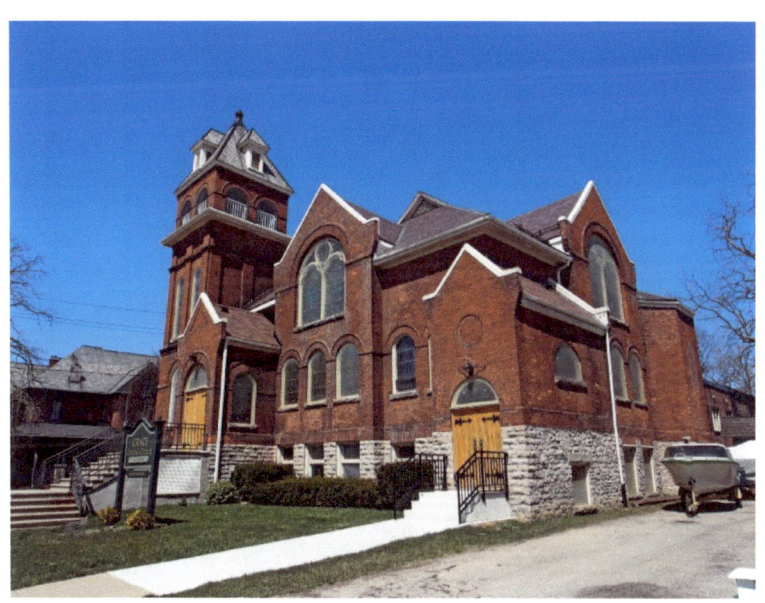

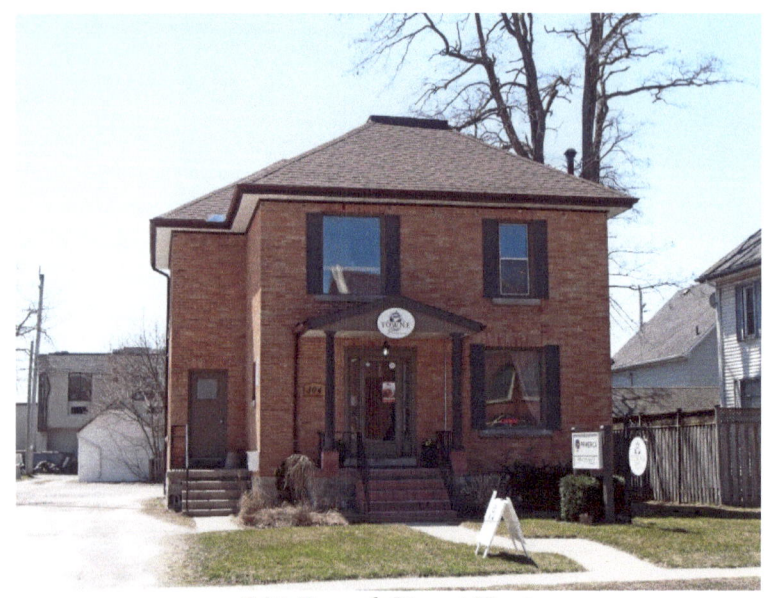

304 Broad Street East

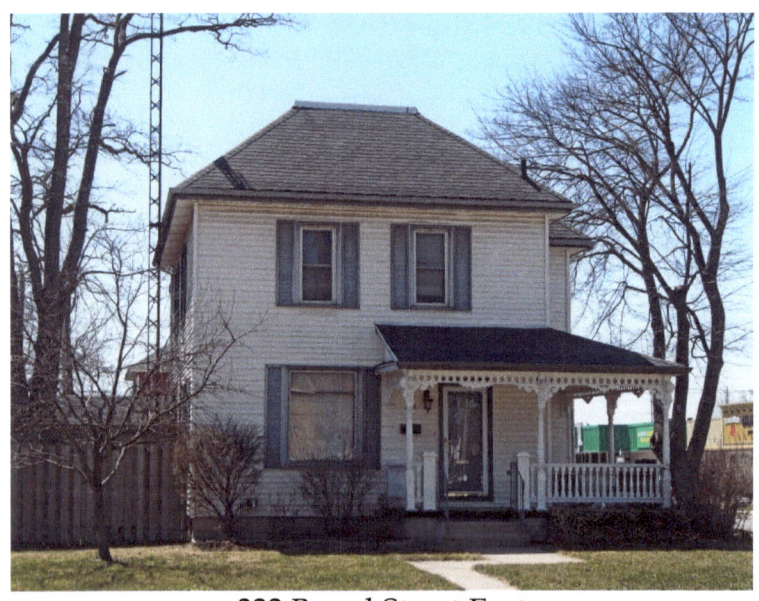

222 Broad Street East

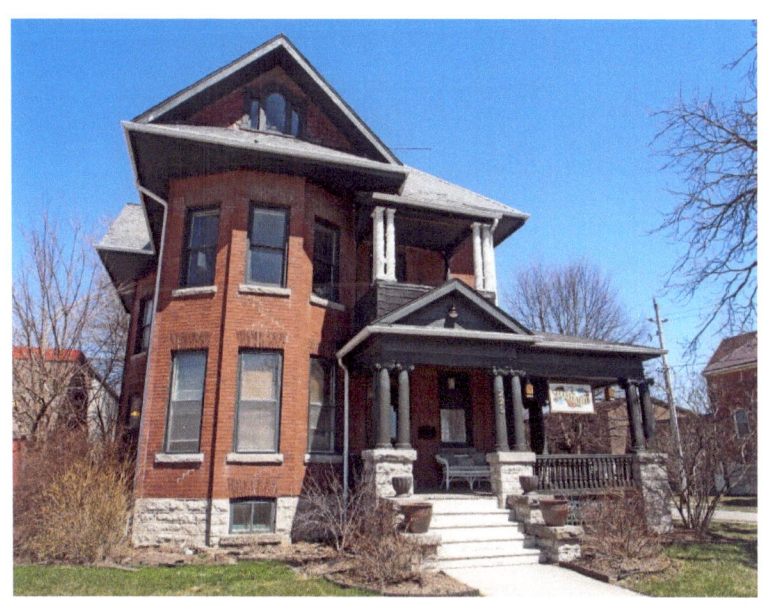

225 Broad Street East

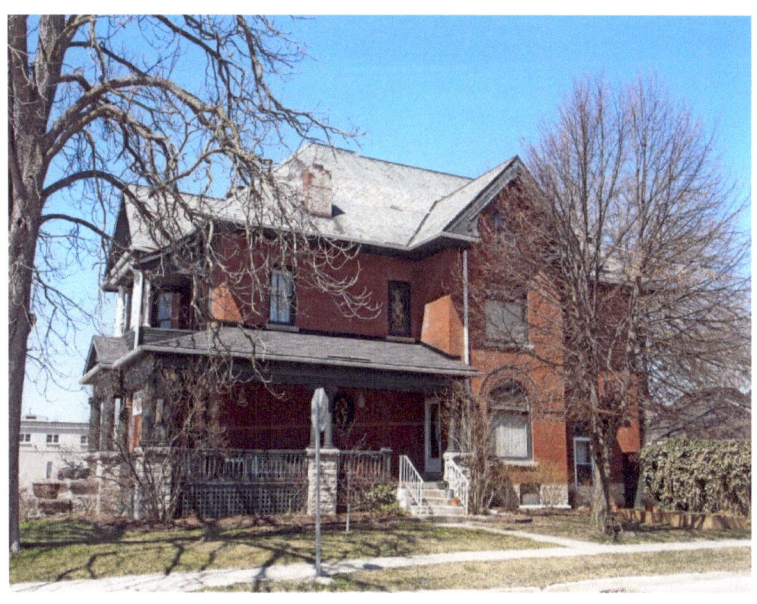

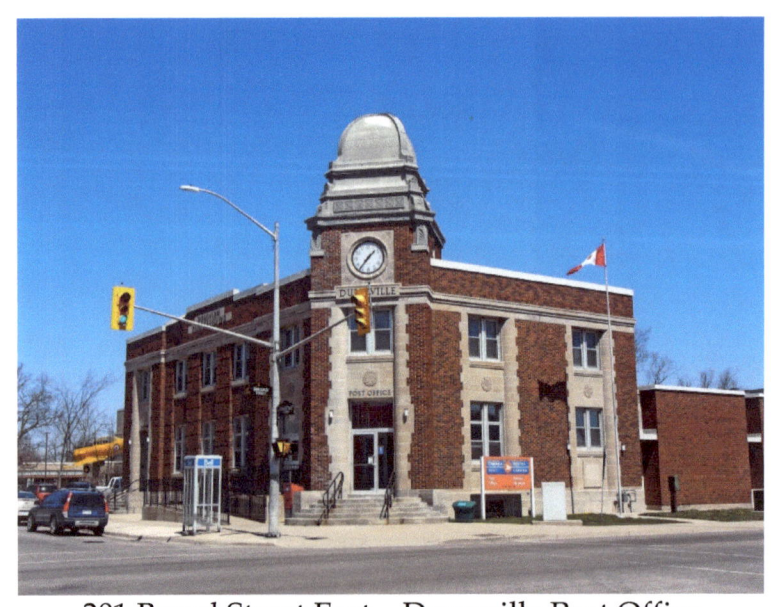

201 Broad Street East – Dunnville Post Office

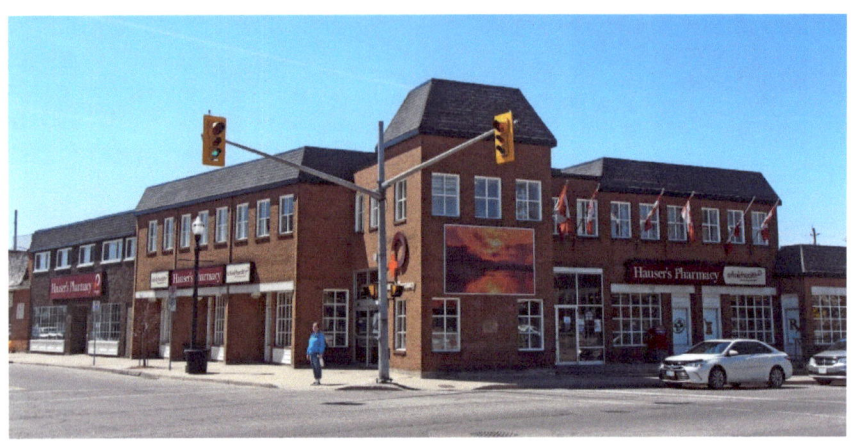

140 Broad Street East

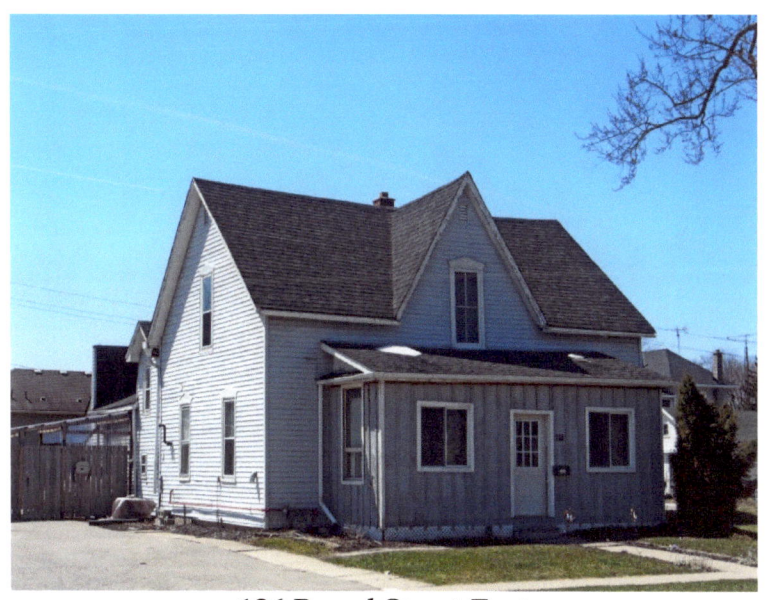

126 Broad Street East

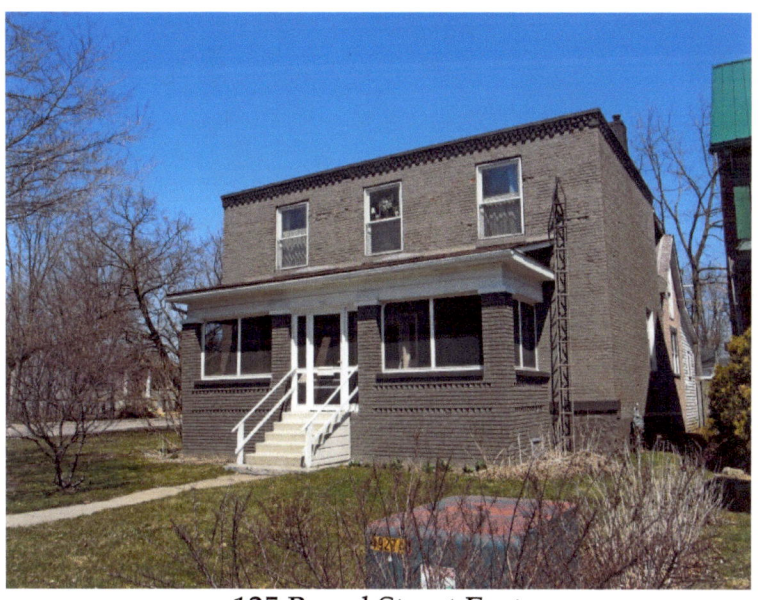

125 Broad Street East

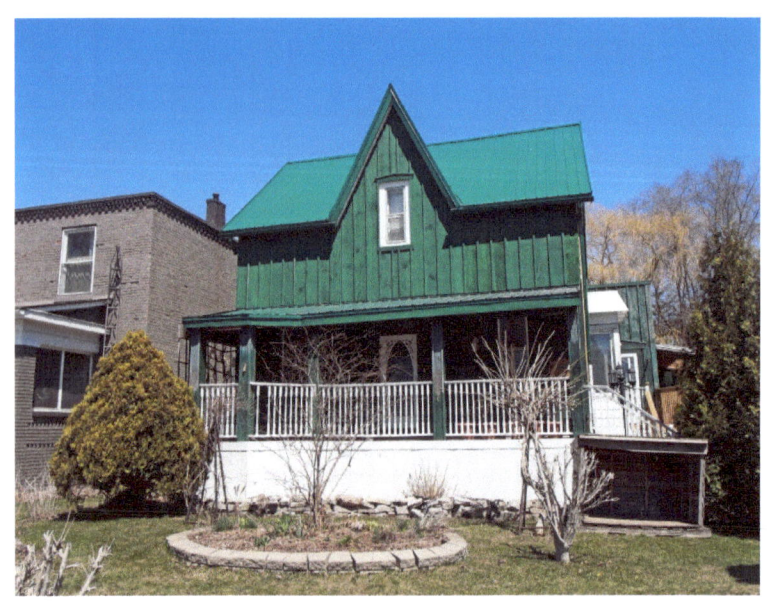

121 Broad Street East

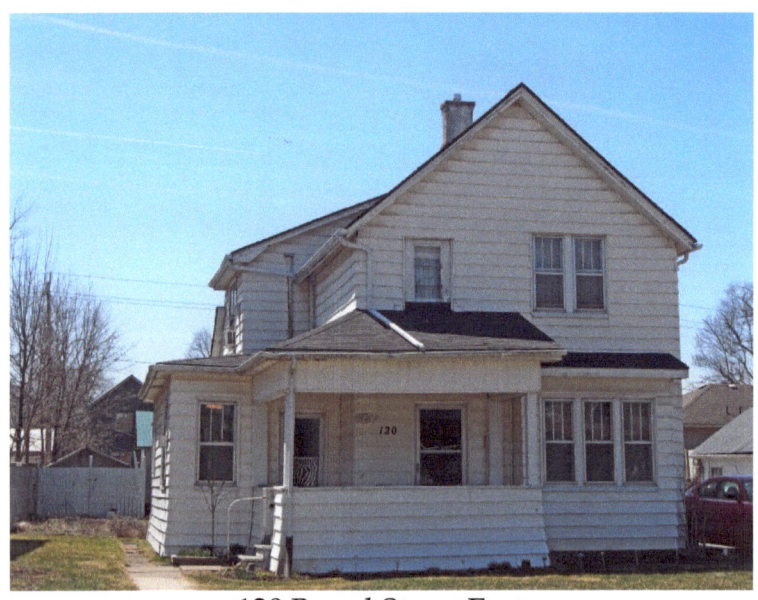

120 Broad Street East

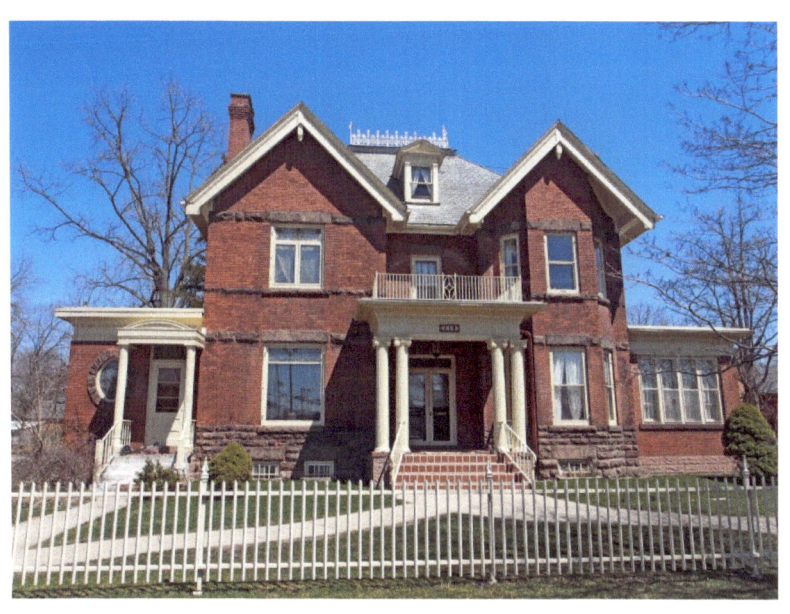

119 Broad Street East

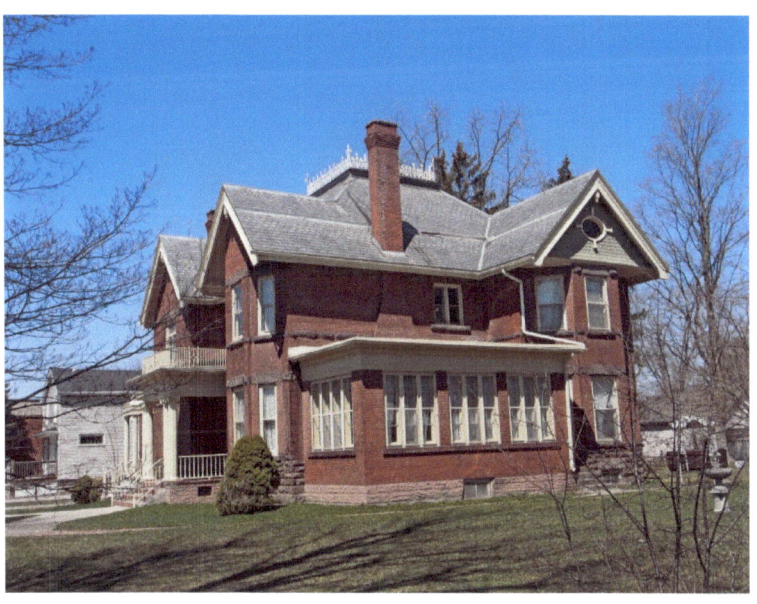

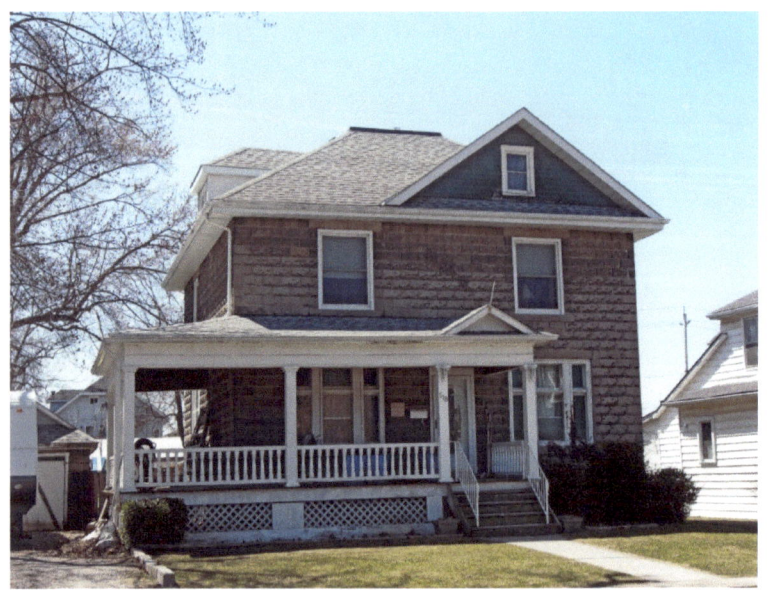

118Broad Street East

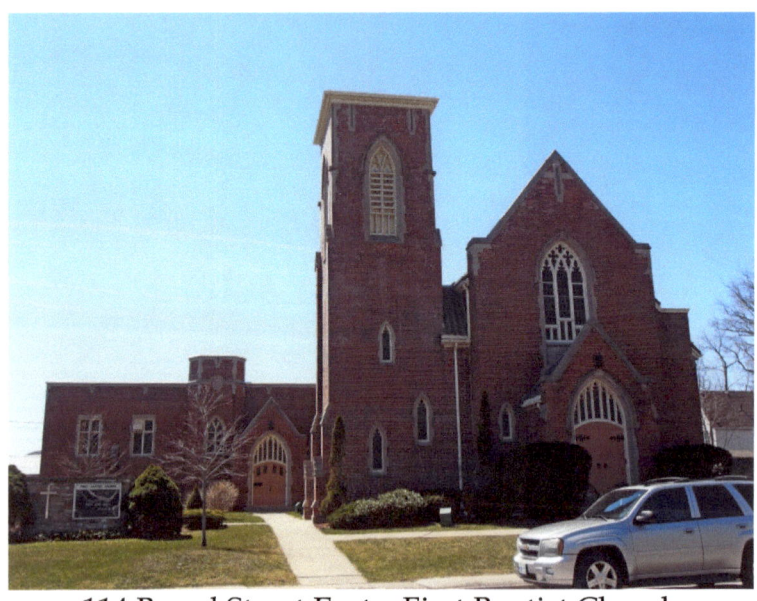

114 Broad Street East – First Baptist Church

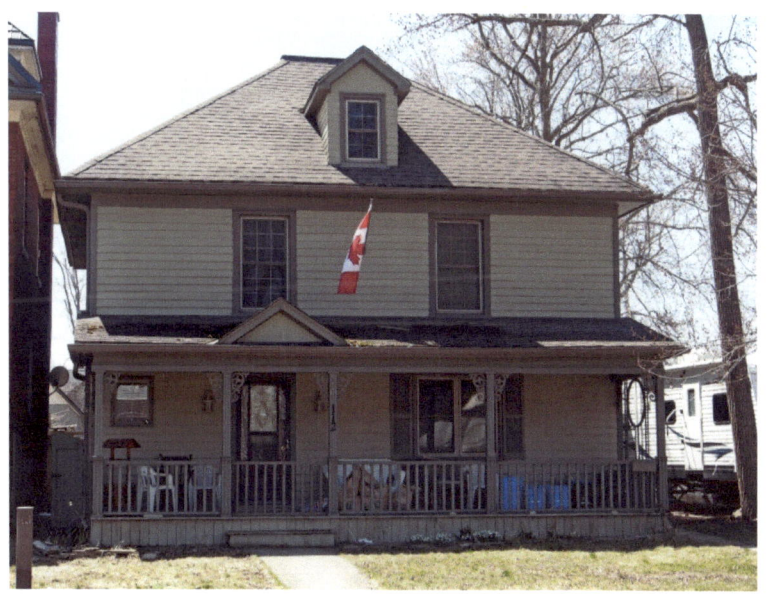

112 Broad Street East

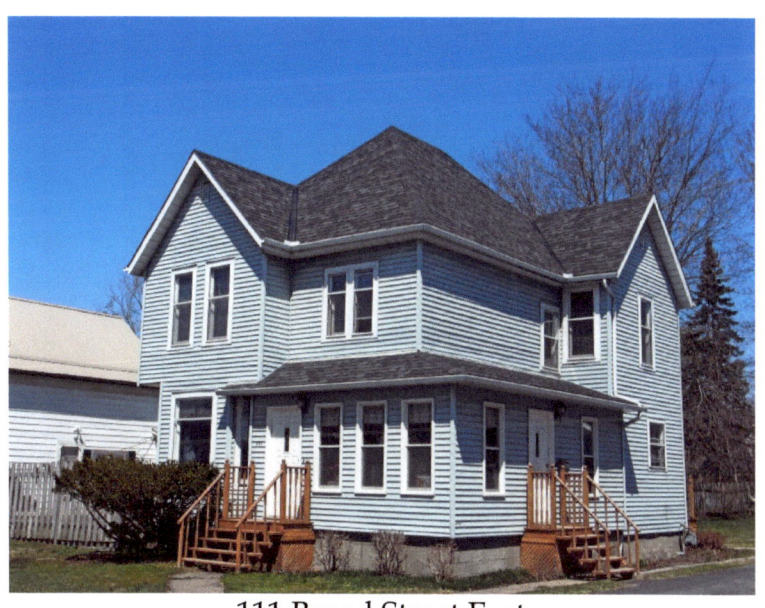

111 Broad Street East

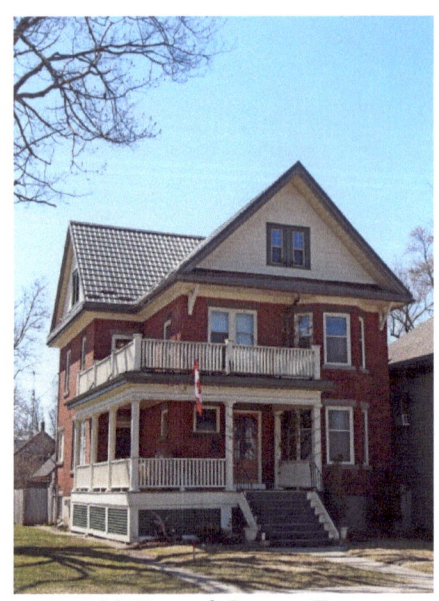

108 Broad Street East

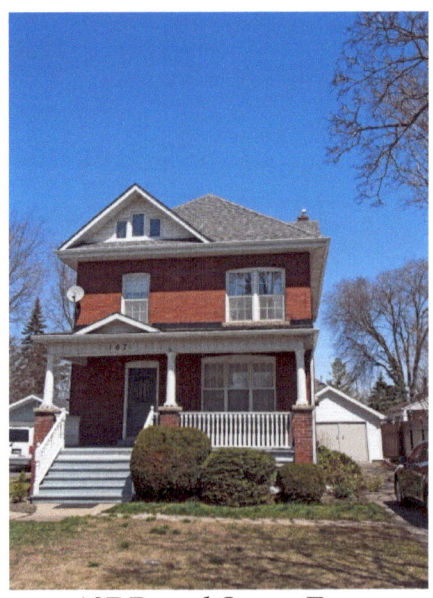

107 Broad Street East

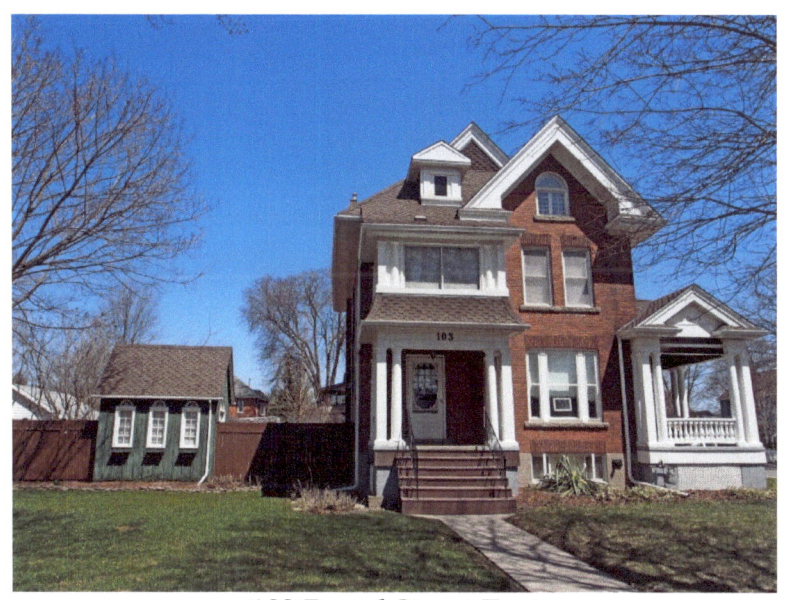

103 Broad Street East

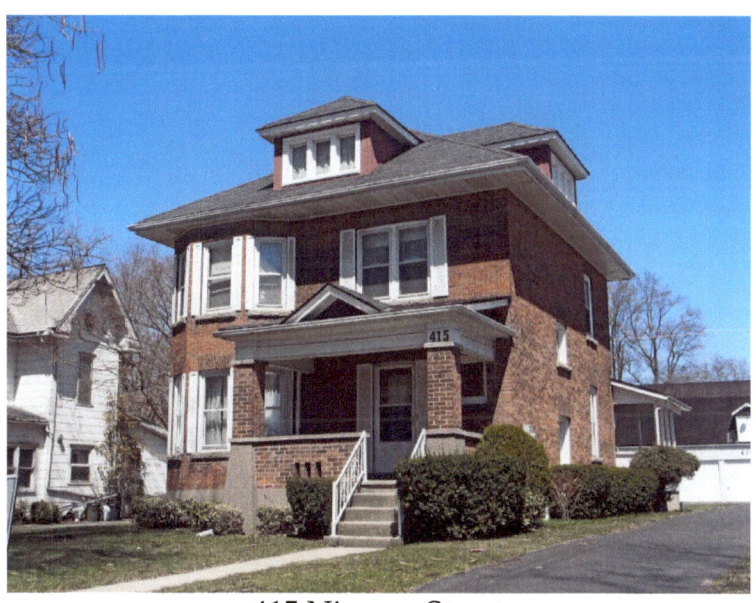

415 Niagara Street

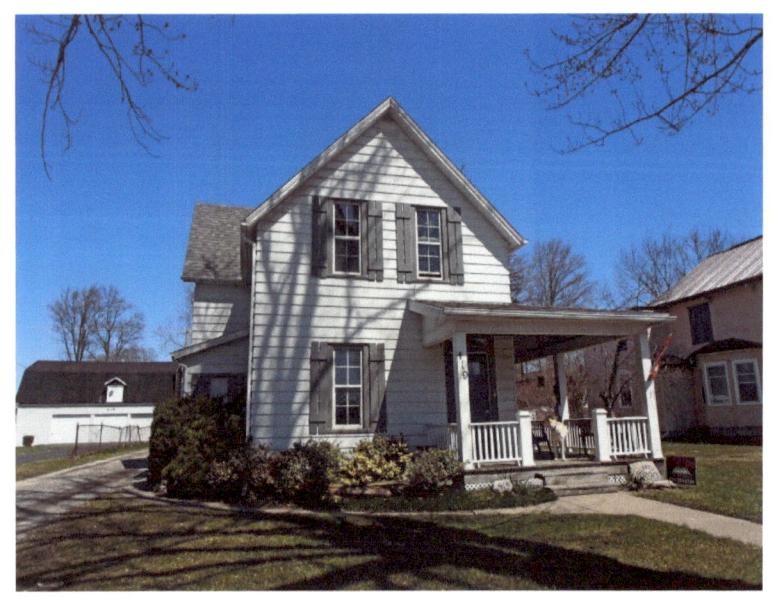

419 Niagara Street

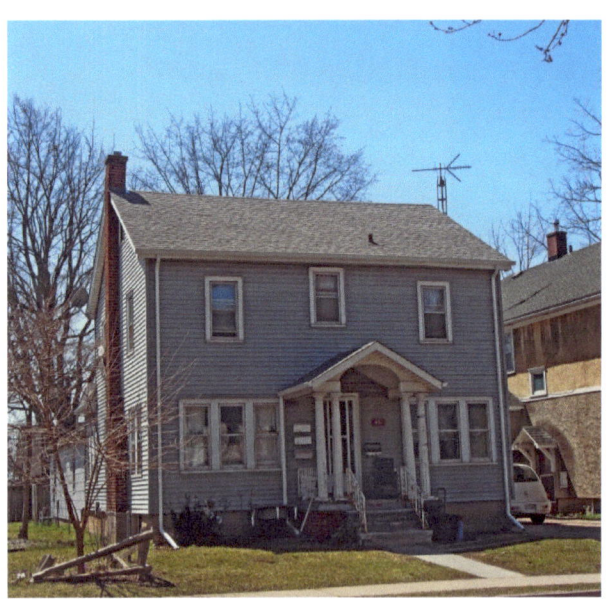

410 Niagara Street

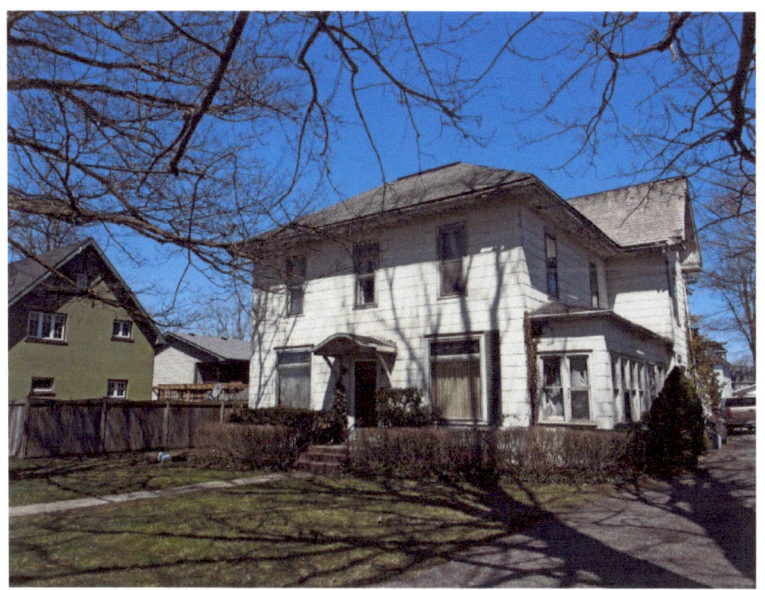

409 Niagara Street

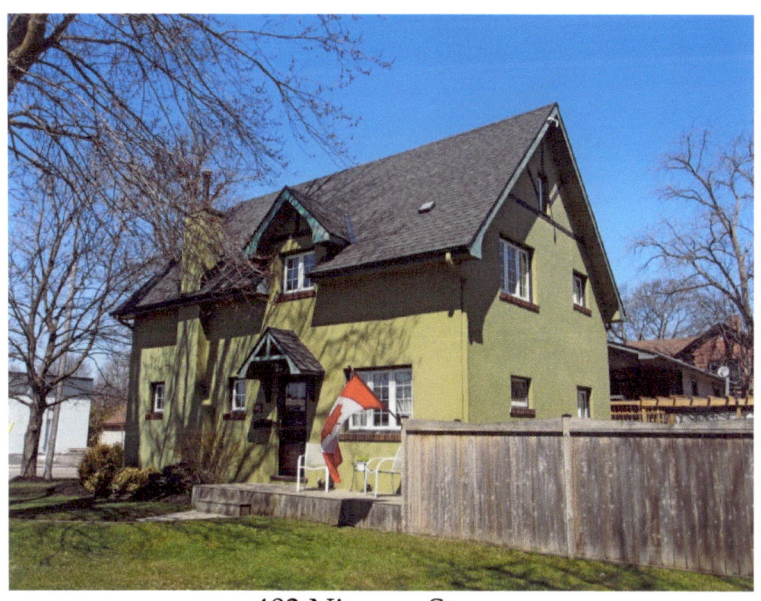

403 Niagara Street

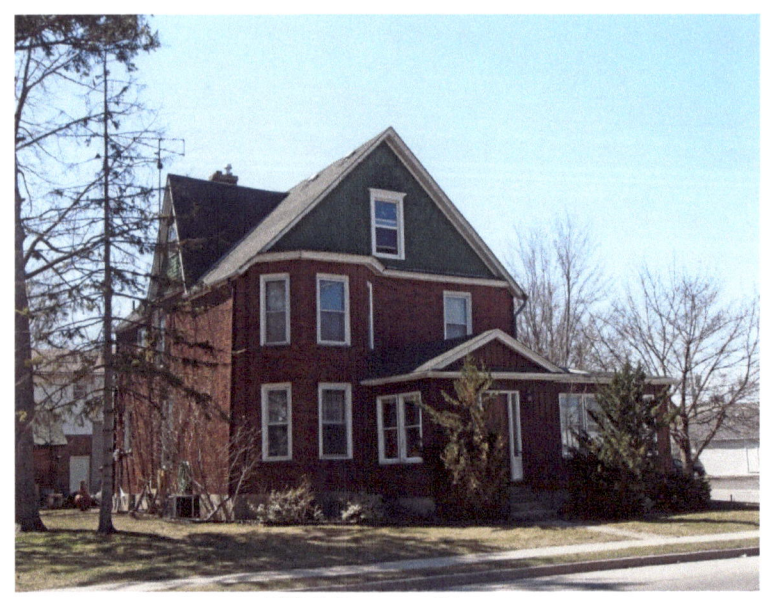

402 Niagara Street

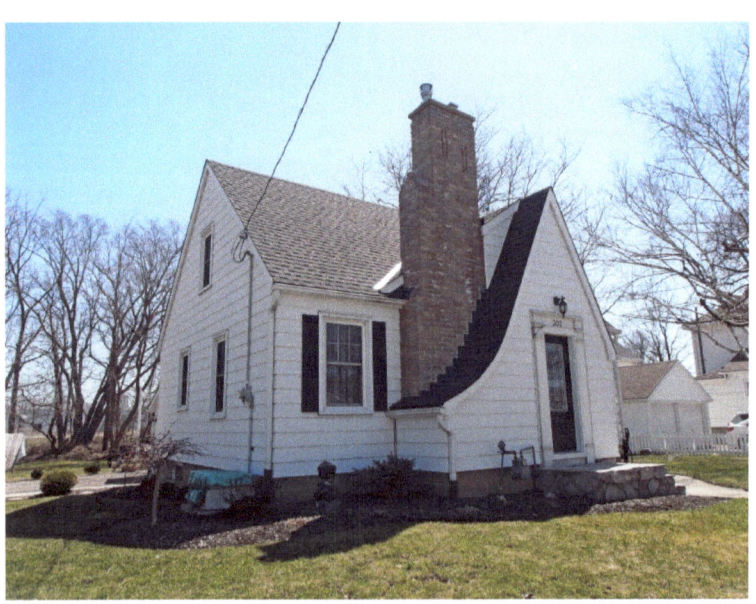

307 Niagara Street

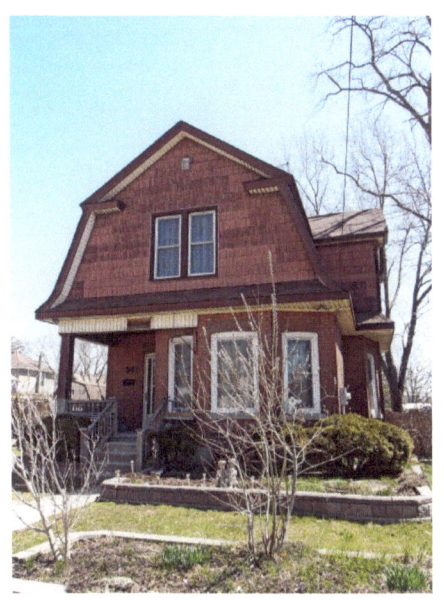

307 Tamarac Street

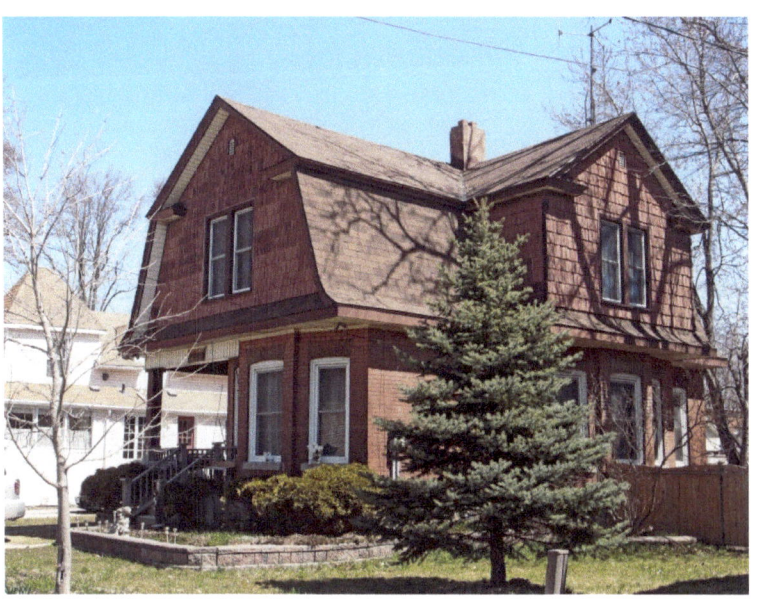

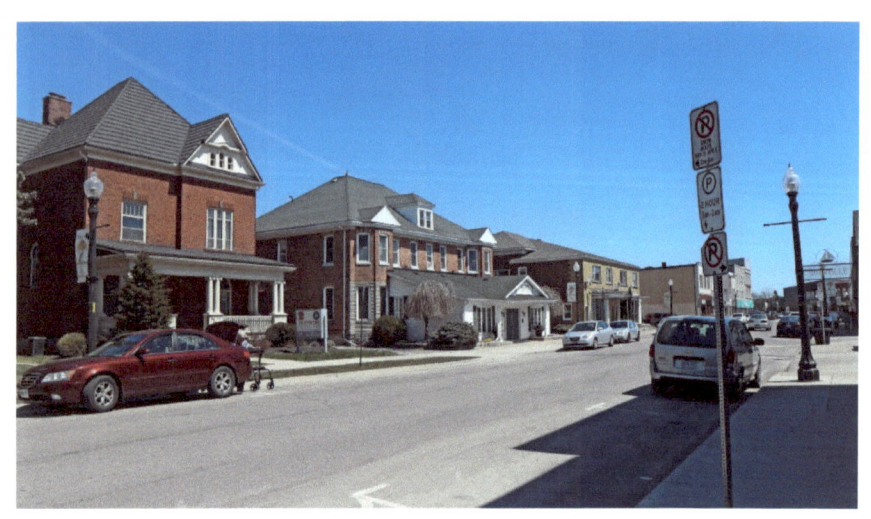

Lock Street

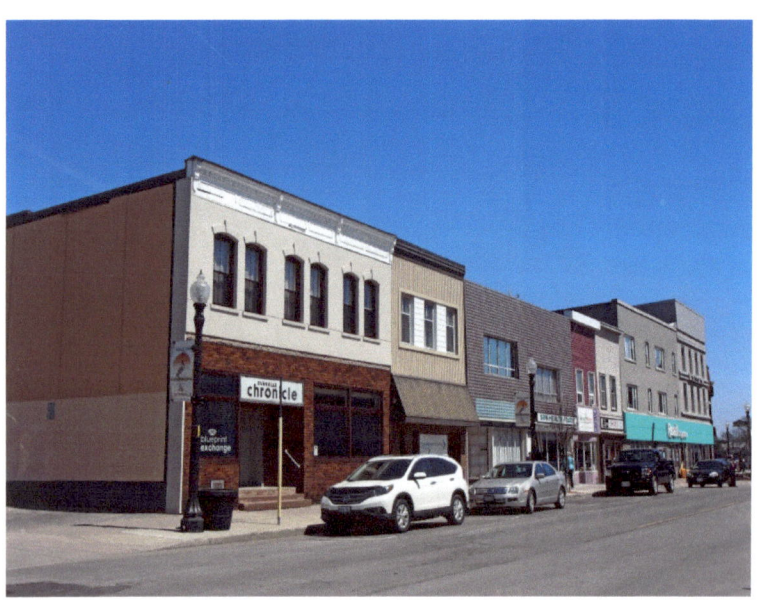

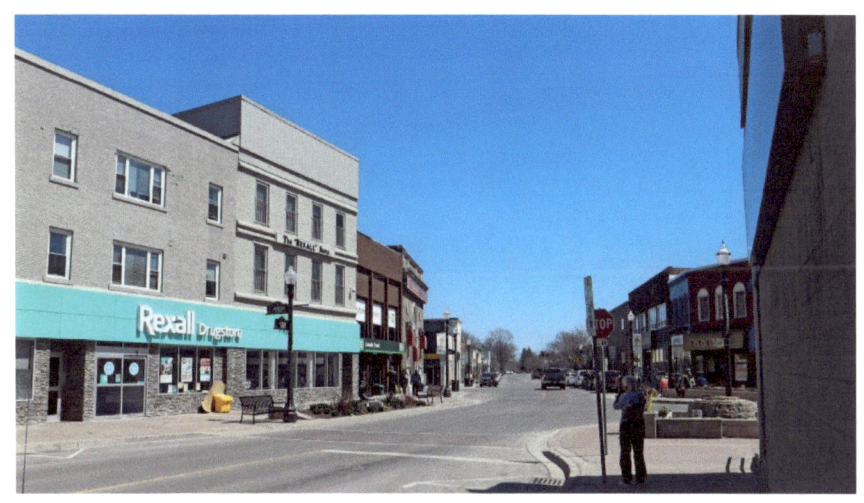

Lock Street

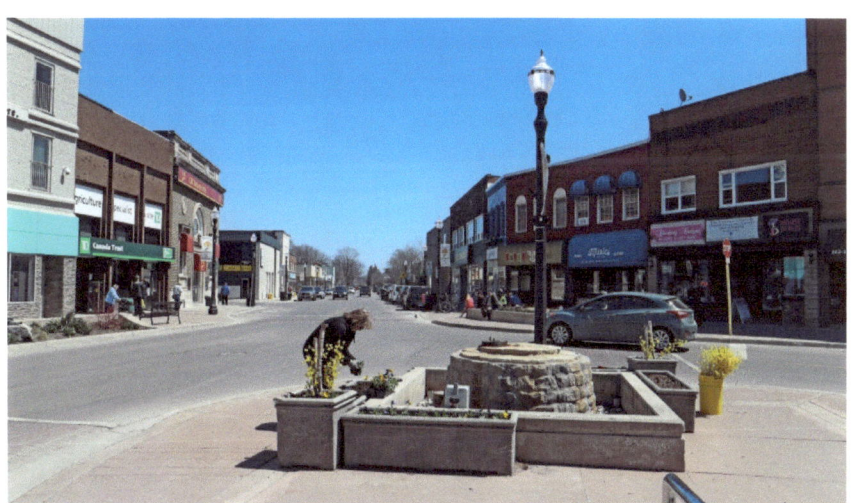

Lock Street

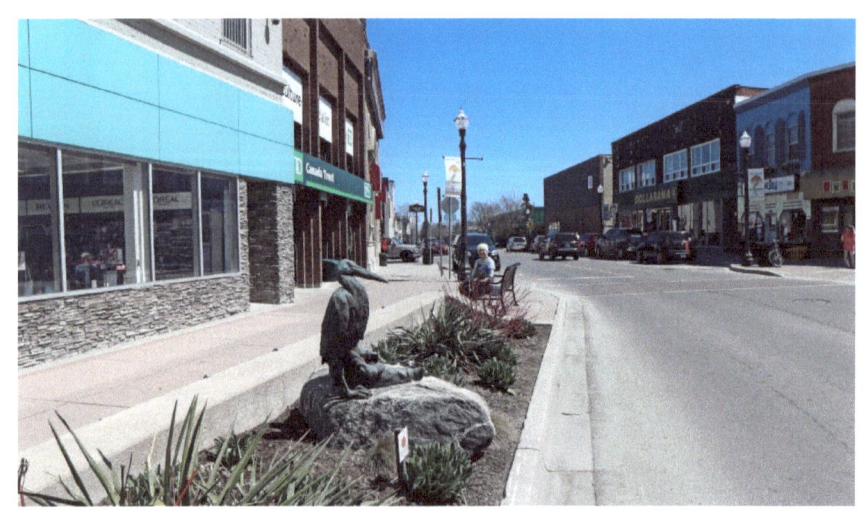

Lock Street

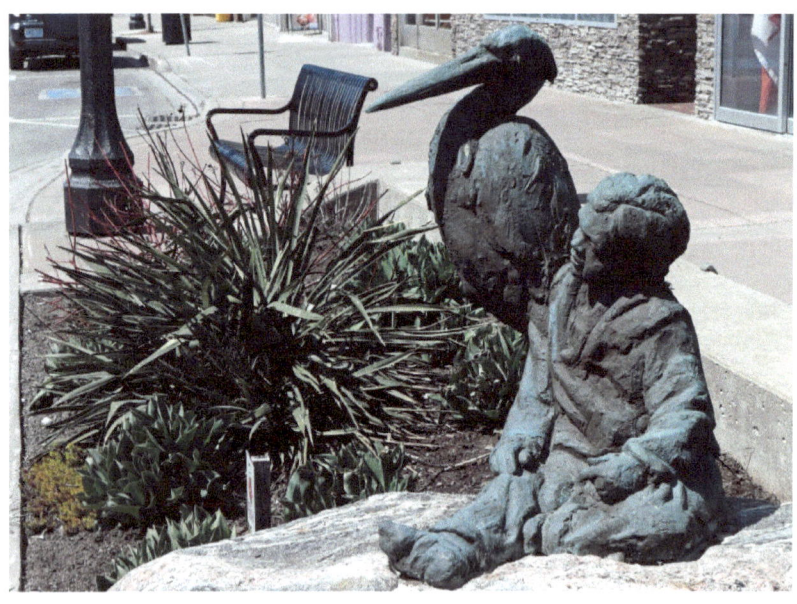

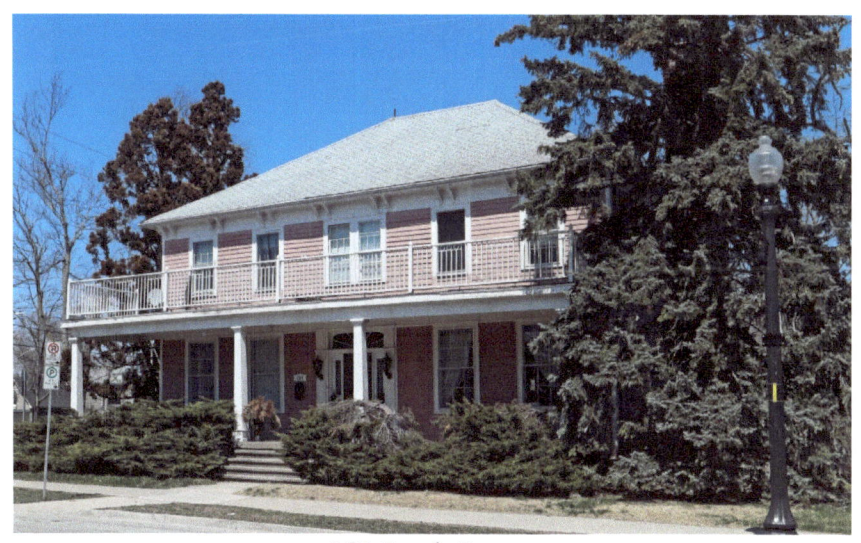

101 Lock Street

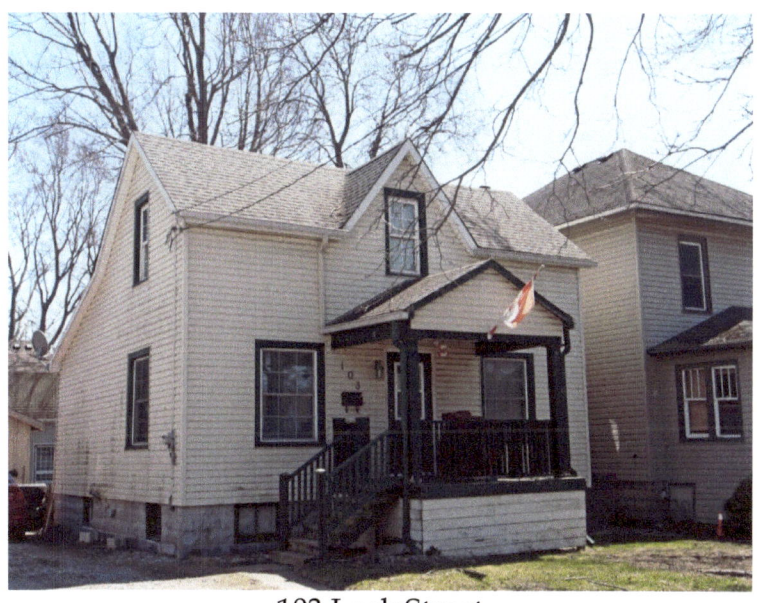

103 Lock Street

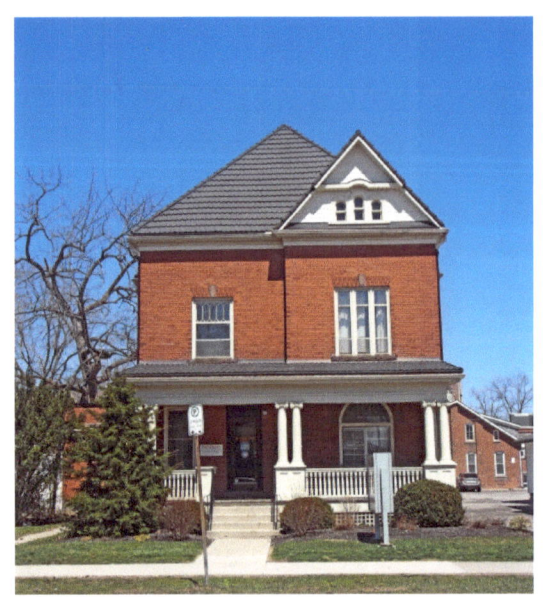

105 Lock Street

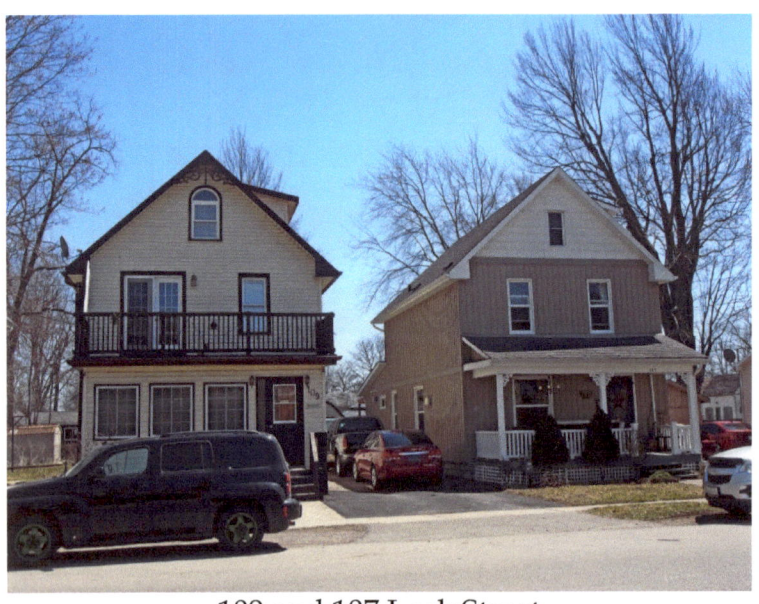

109 and 107 Lock Street

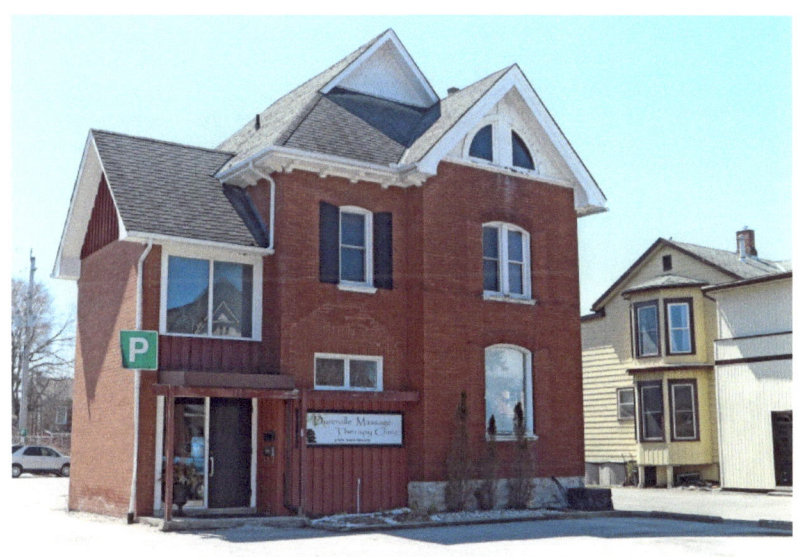

110 Lock Street

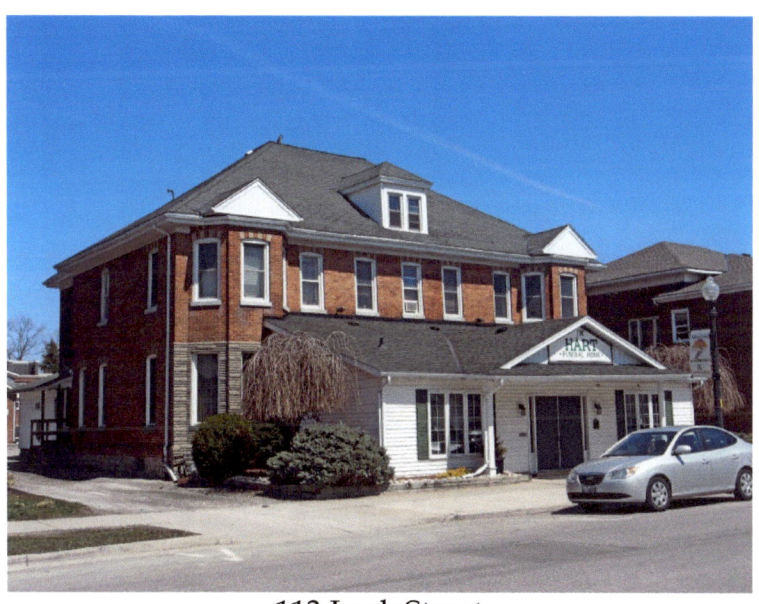

113 Lock Street

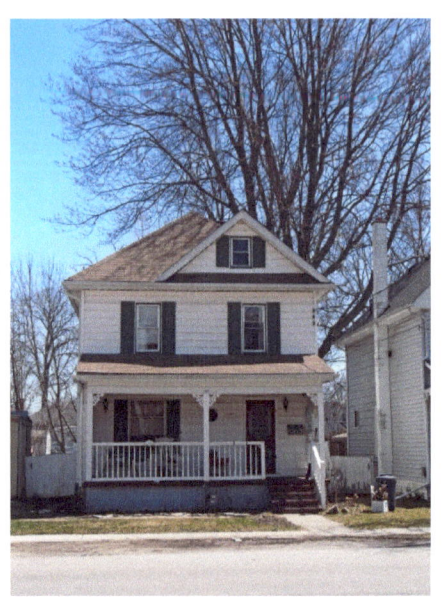

115 Lock Street

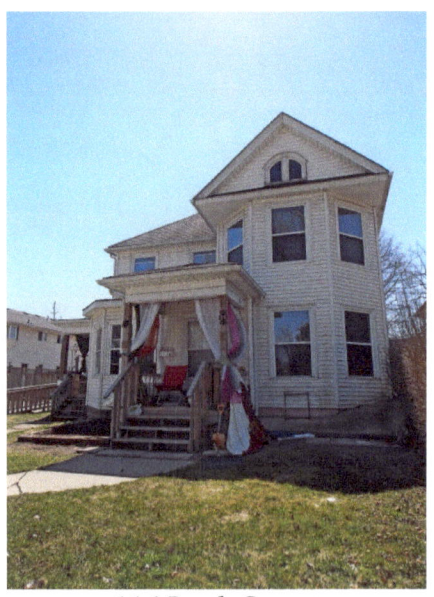

116 Lock Street

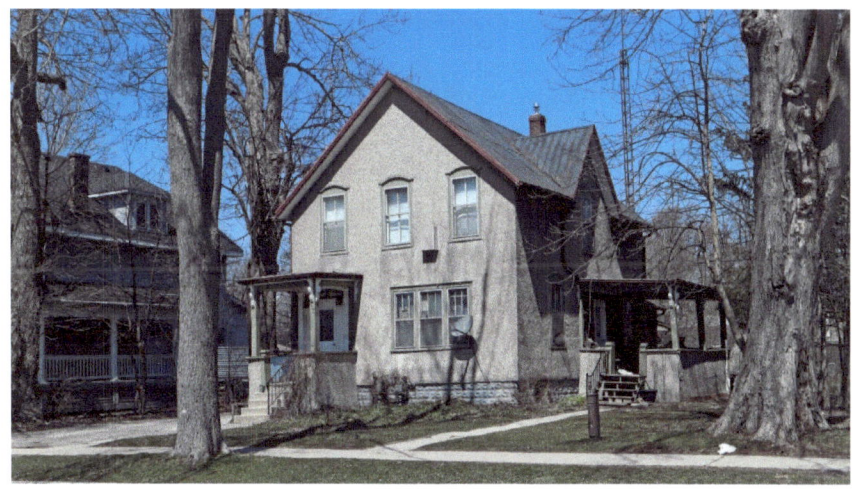

117 Lock Street

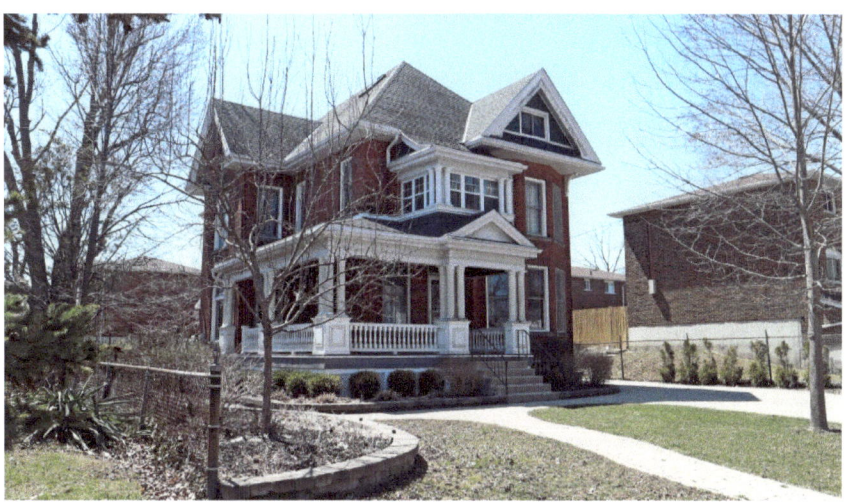

Lock Street

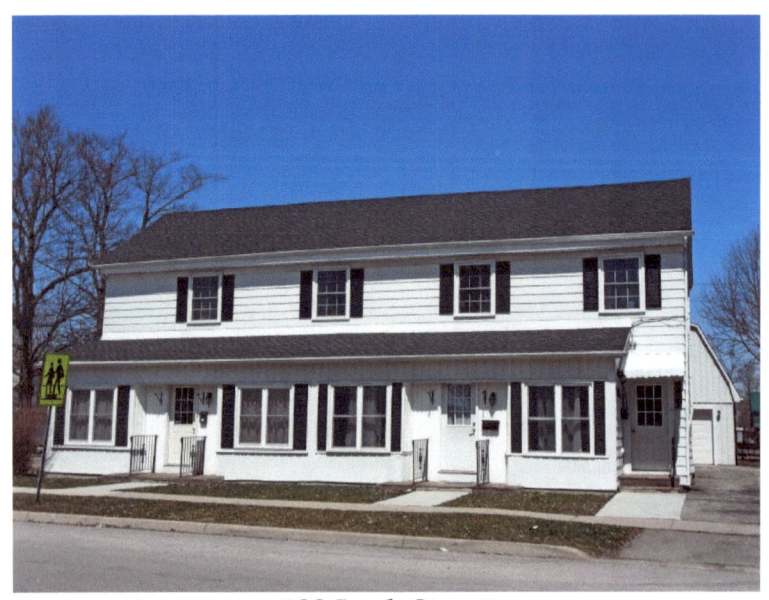

133 Lock Street

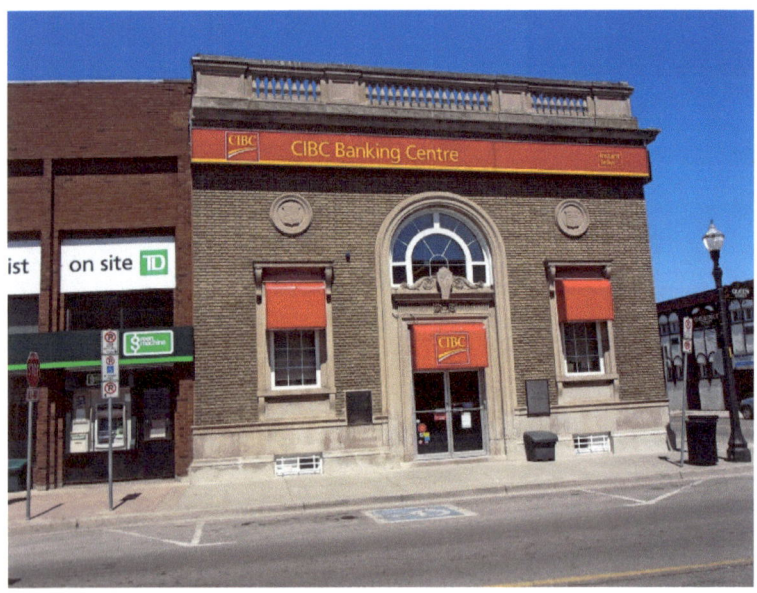

165 Lock Street

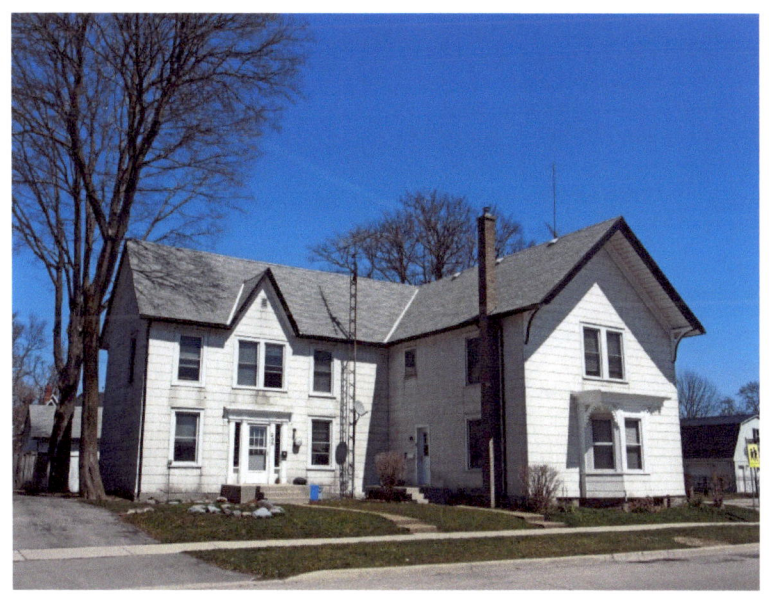

205 Lock Street

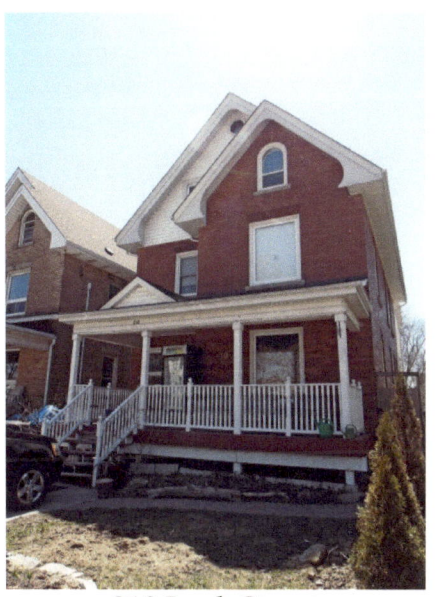

210 Lock Street

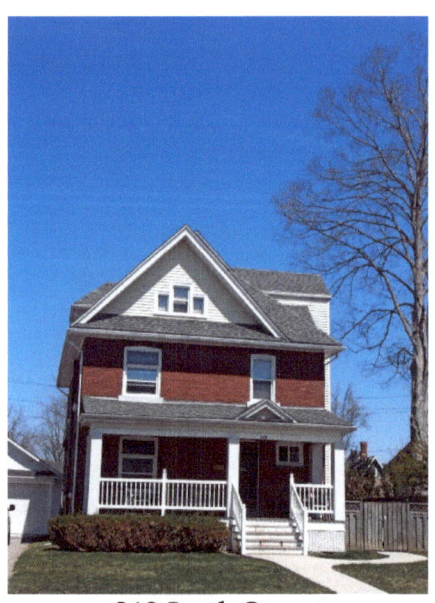

213 Lock Street

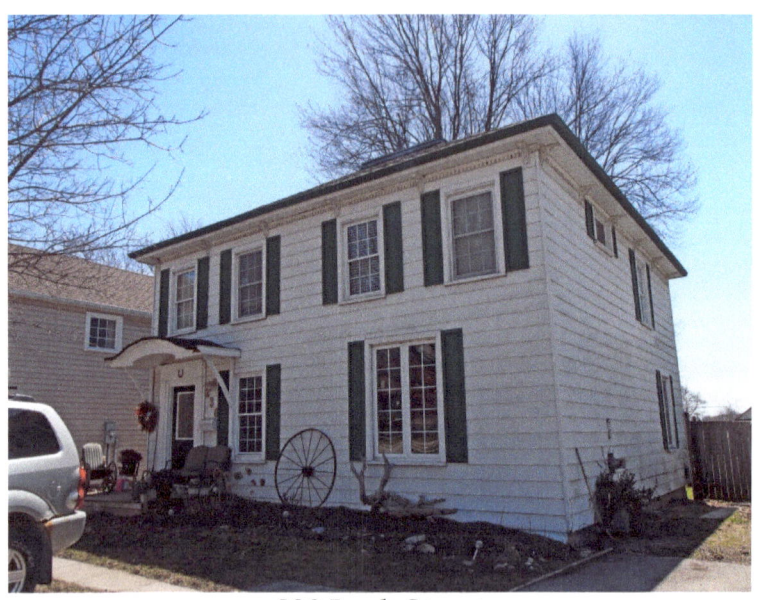

230 Lock Street

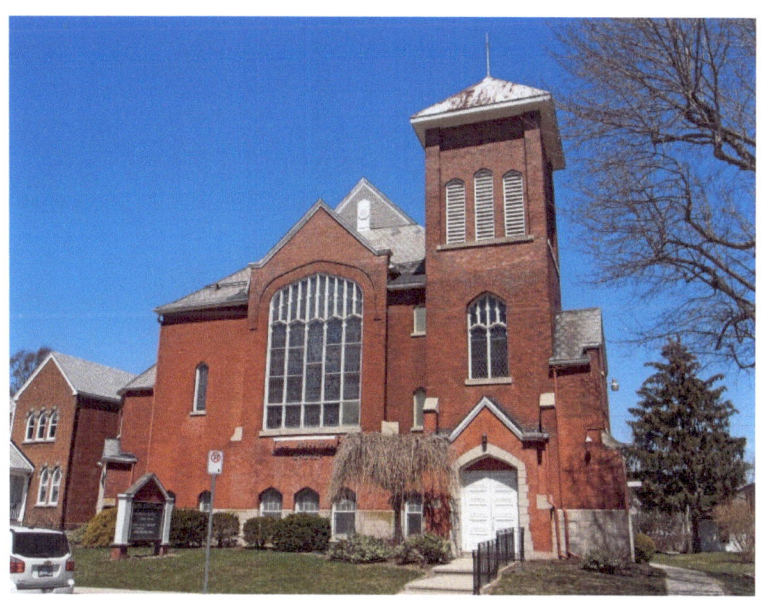

223 Lock Street West – Knox Presbyterian Church

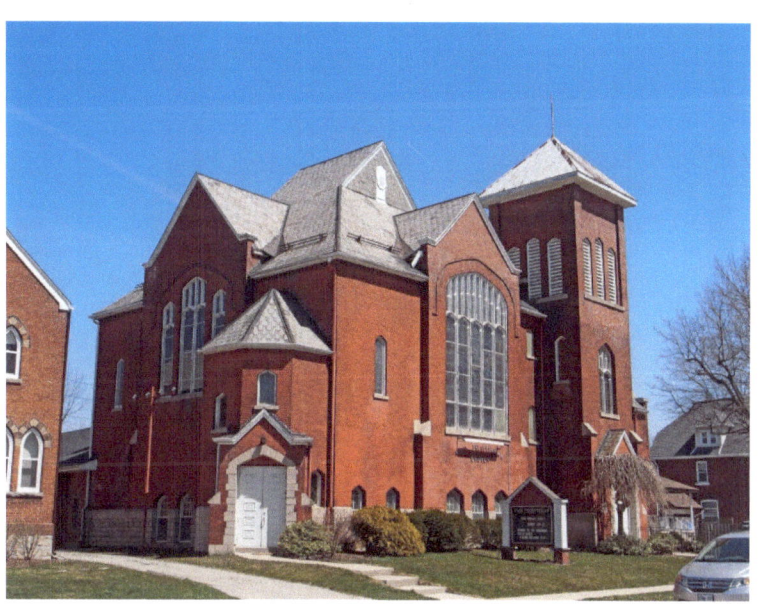

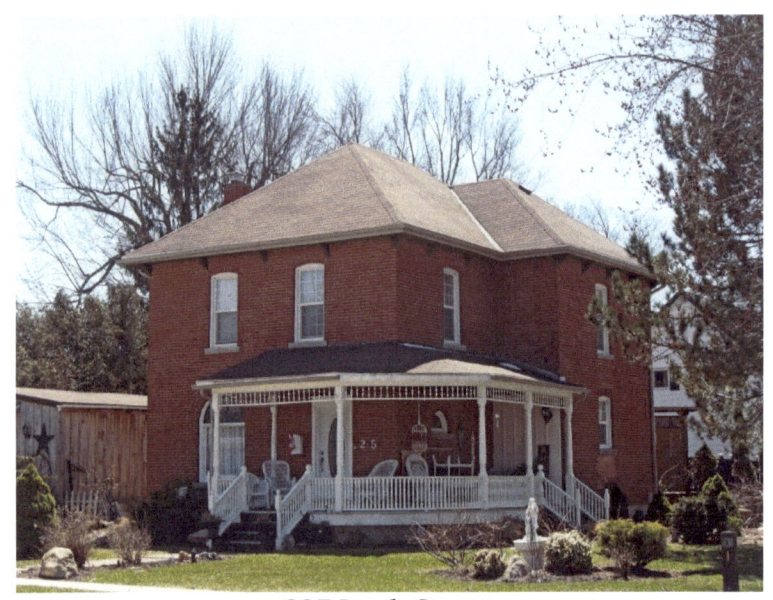

225 Lock Street

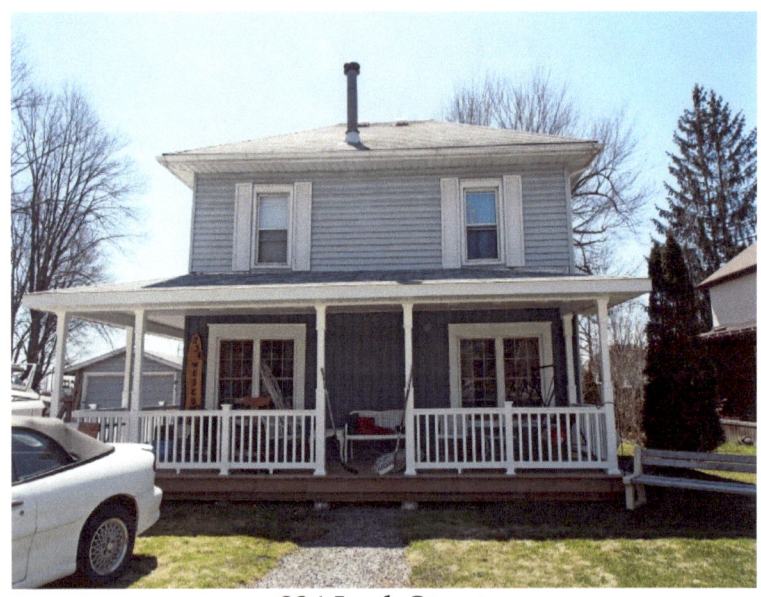

234 Lock Street

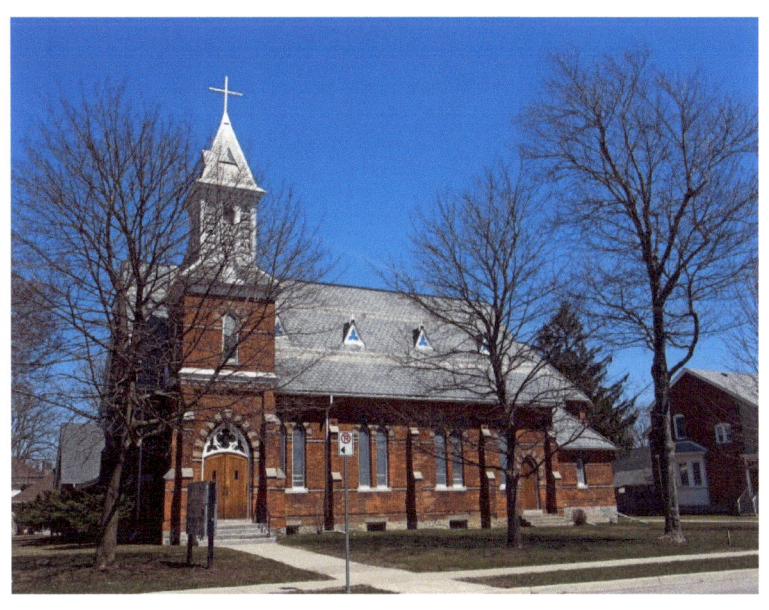

233 Lock Street West – St. Paul's Anglican Church

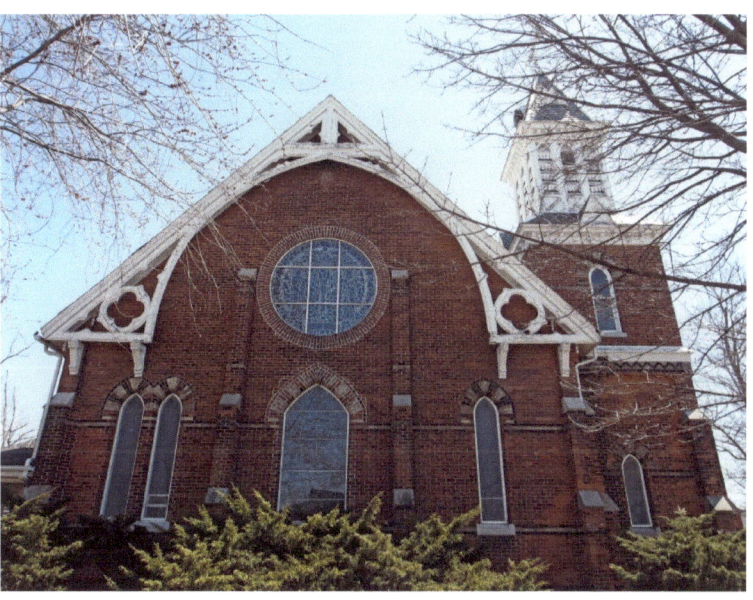

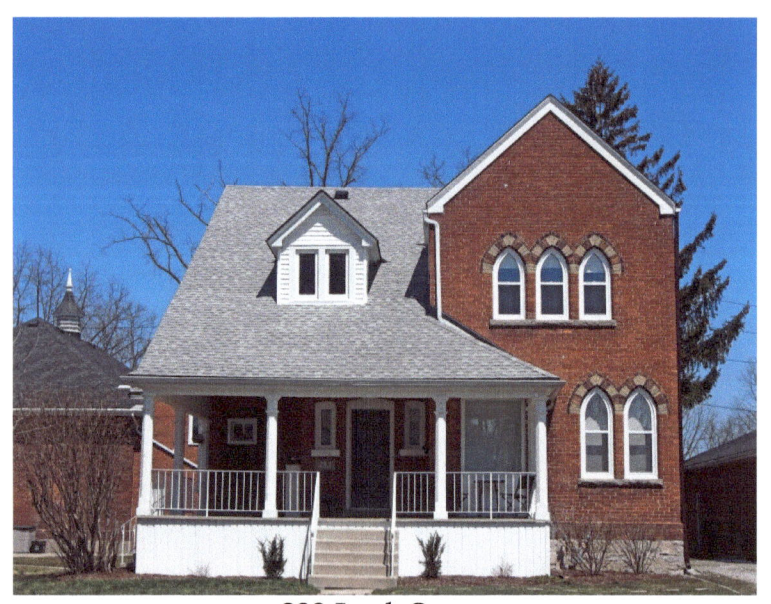

233 Lock Street

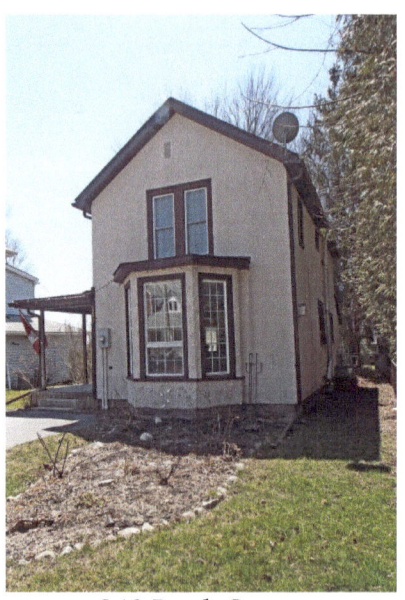

240 Lock Street

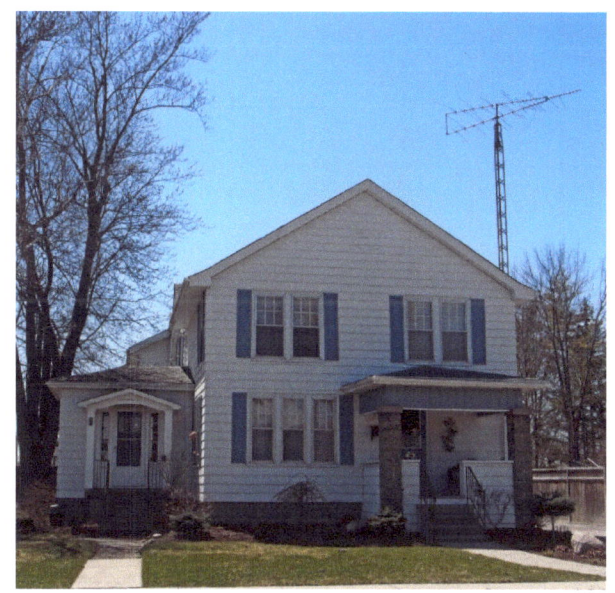

304 Lock Street

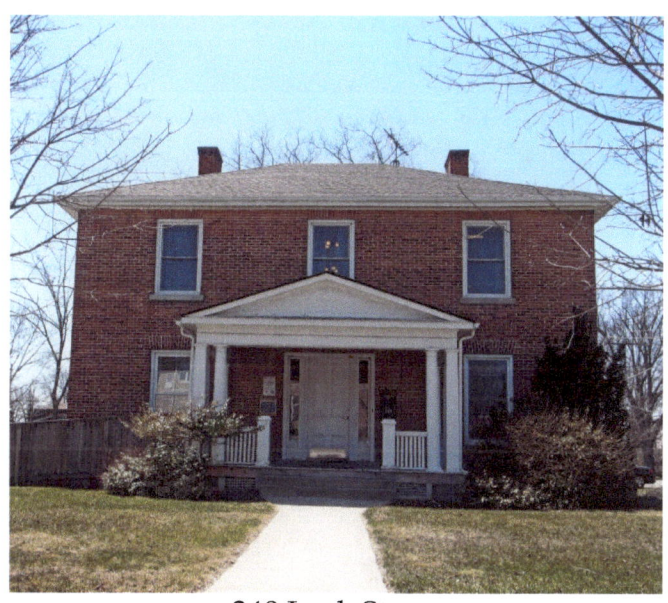

340 Lock Street

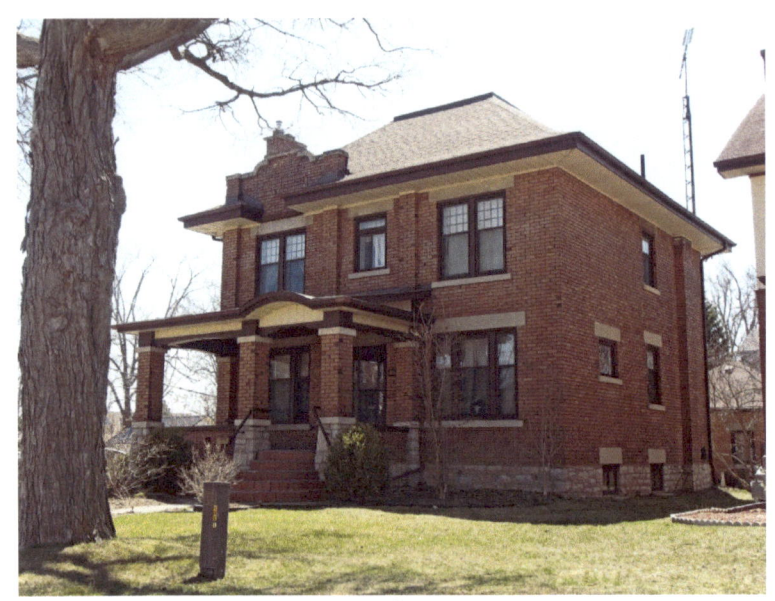

404 Lock Street

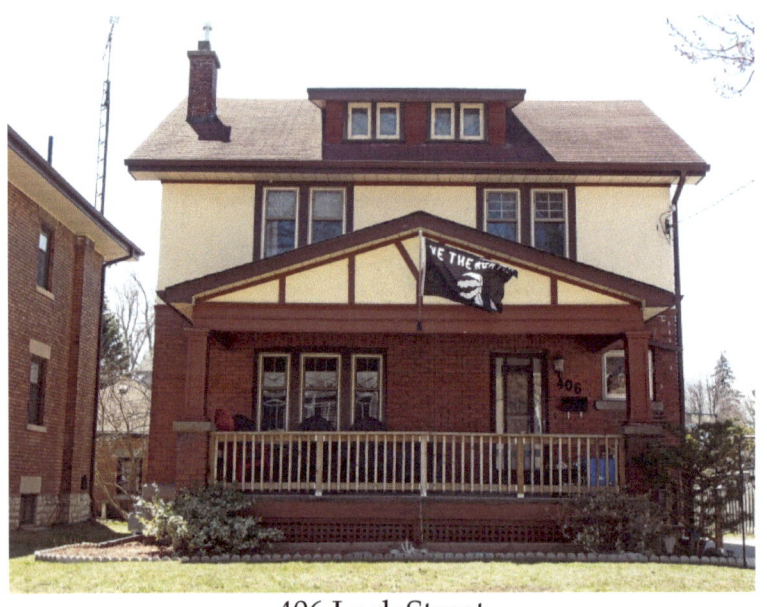

406 Lock Street

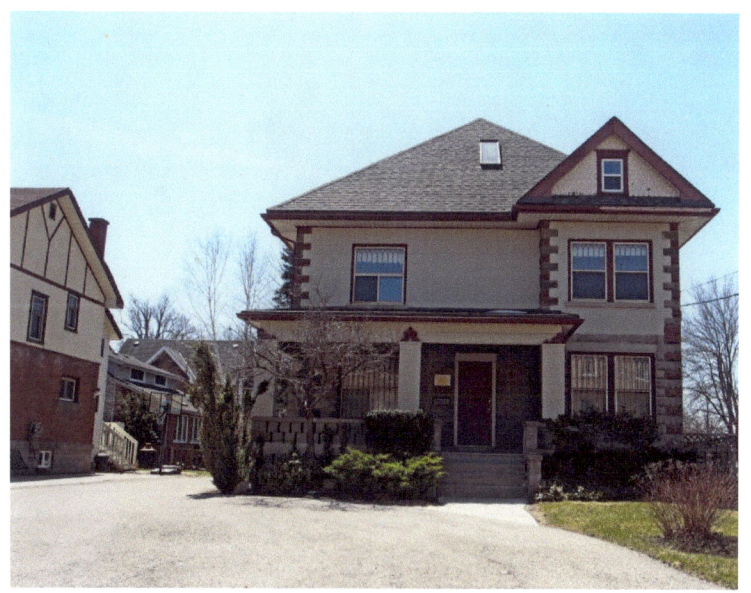

410 Lock Street

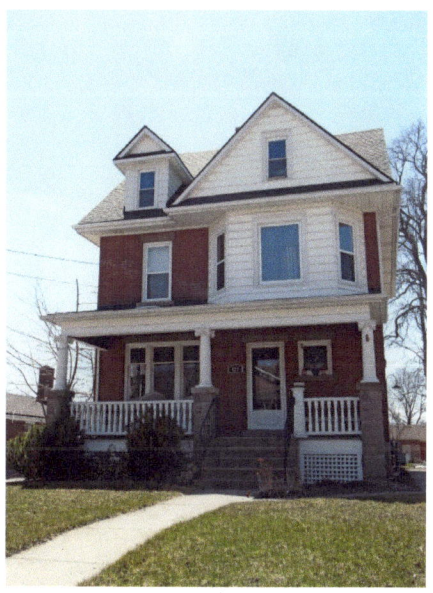

422 Lock Street

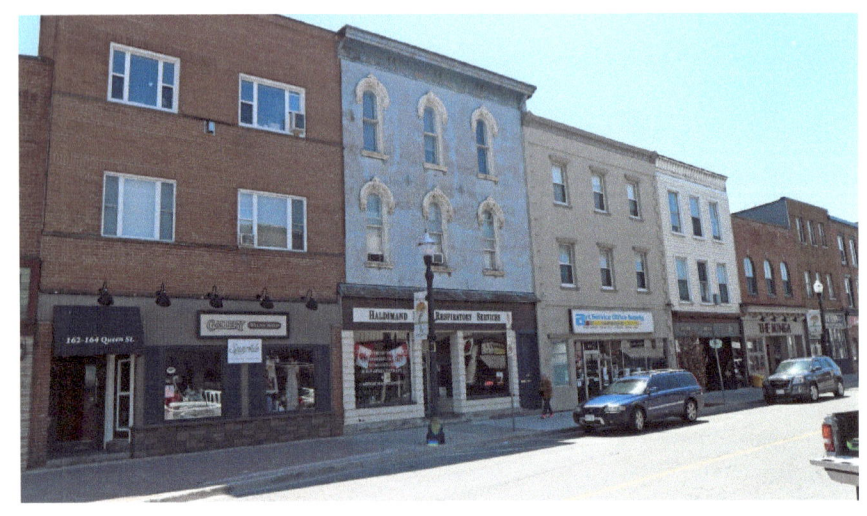

Queen Street

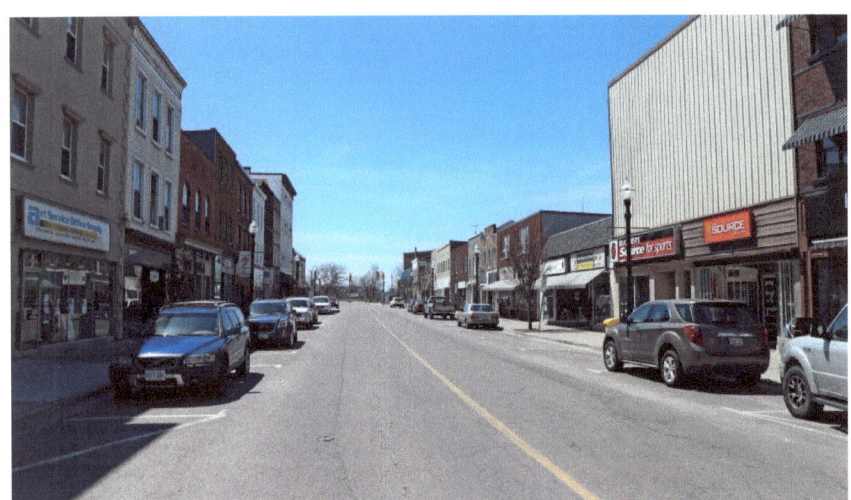

Queen Street

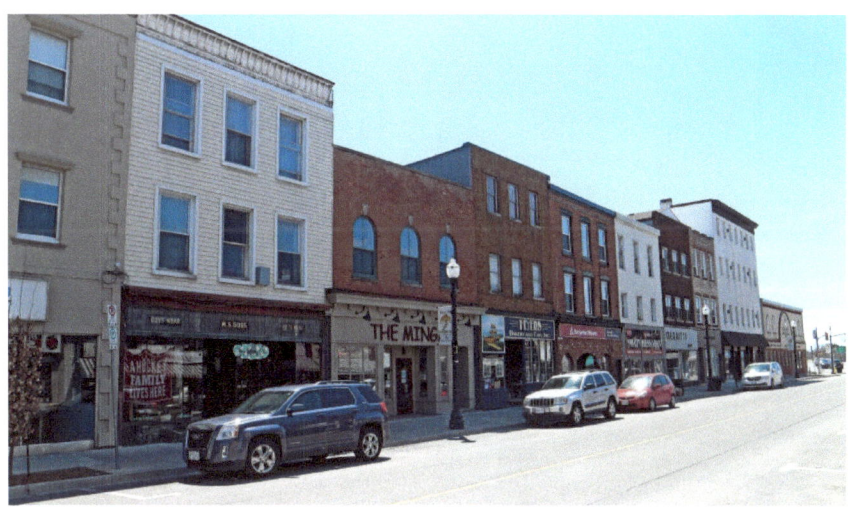

Queen Street

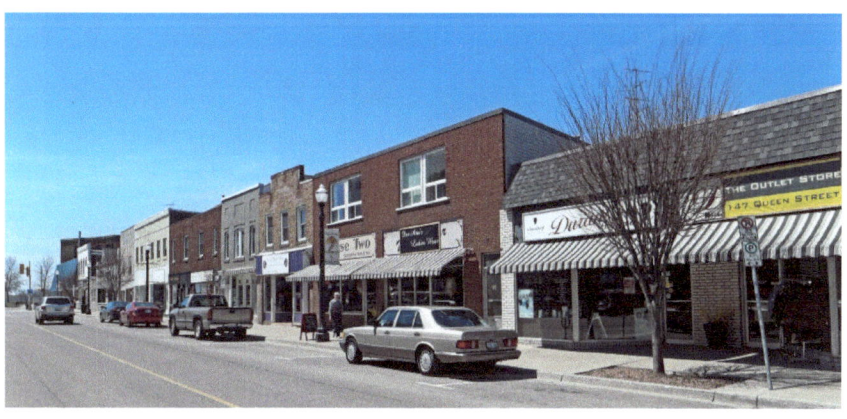

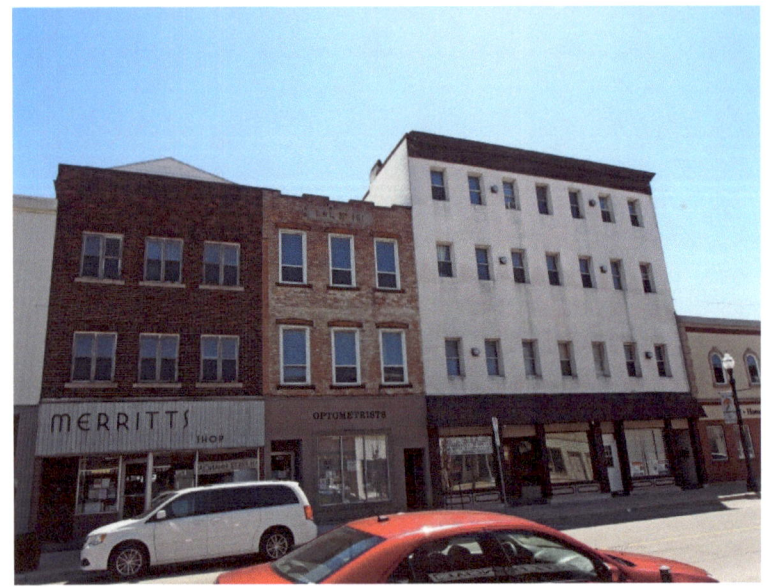

132-134 Queen Street

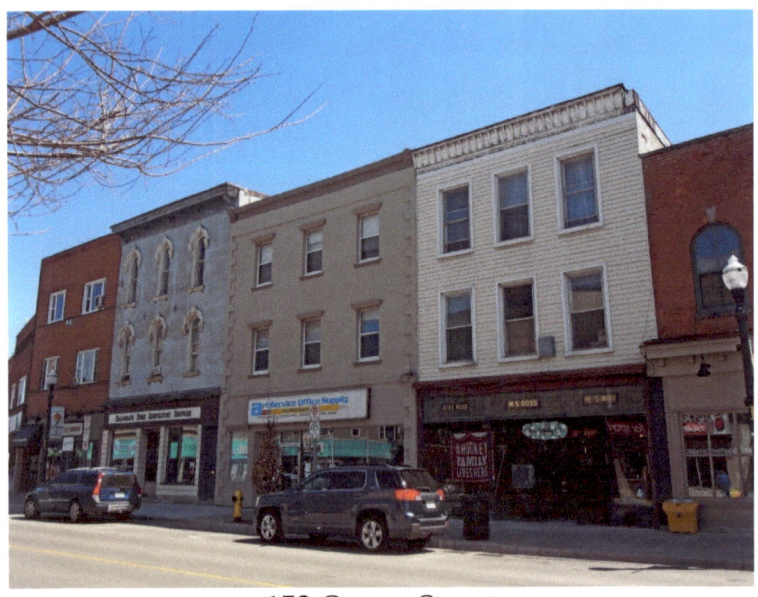

152 Queen Street

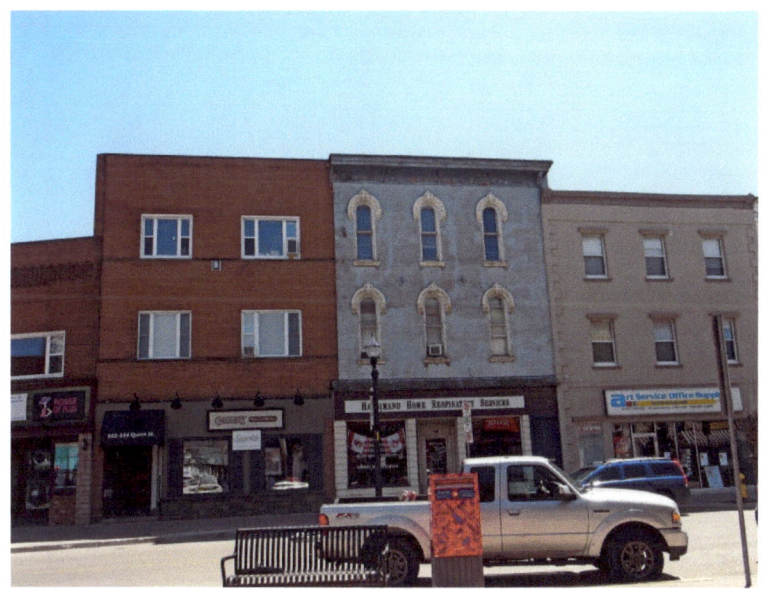

162-164 Queen Street

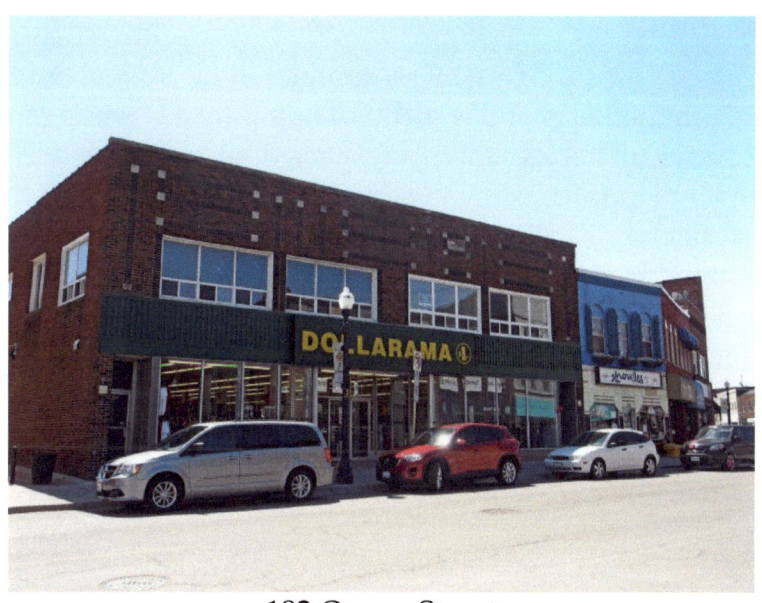

182 Queen Street

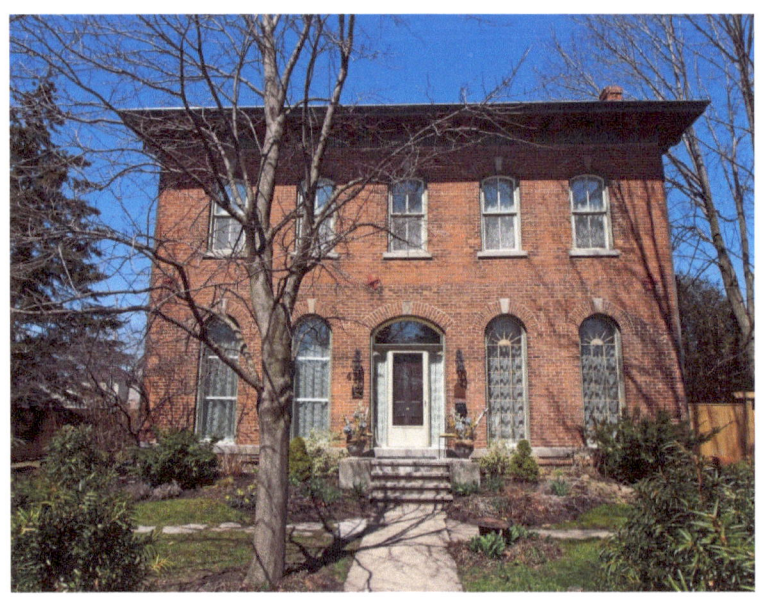

431 Queen Street – George Sime emigrated from Scotland to Canada in the 1840s and settled in Dunnville. He was a tanner and courier by trade; he was a respected businessman and prominent landowner involved in local politics. He built this two-storey home in 1869 in the Italianate style of architecture. The hipped roof has projecting eaves with paired cornice brackets. The keystone above the entrance has a thistle; there are sidelights and a transom surrounding the door. The middle keystone on the upper storey has the date.

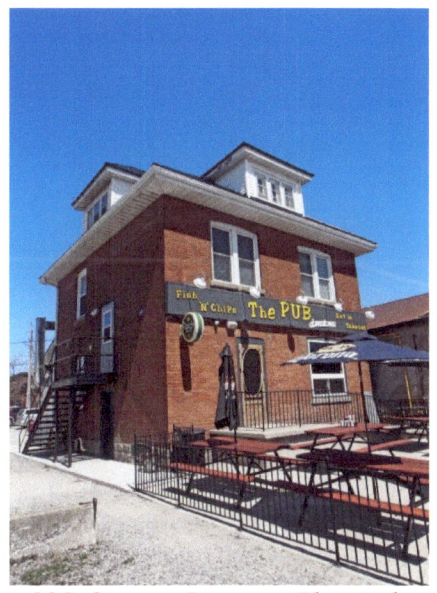

223 Queen Street – The Pub

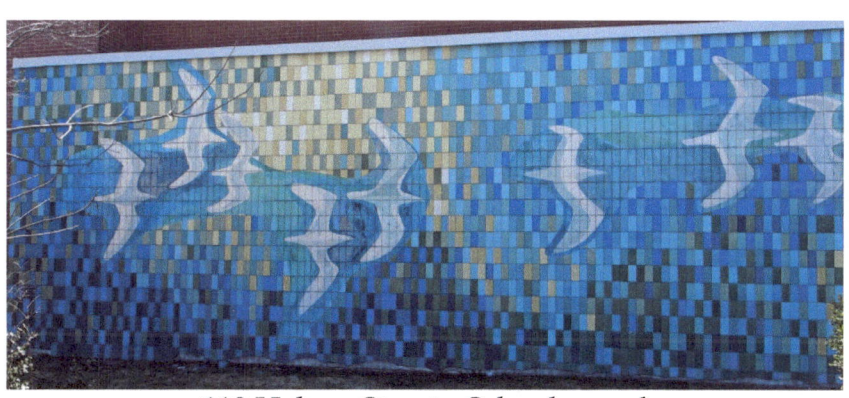

110 Helena Street - School mural

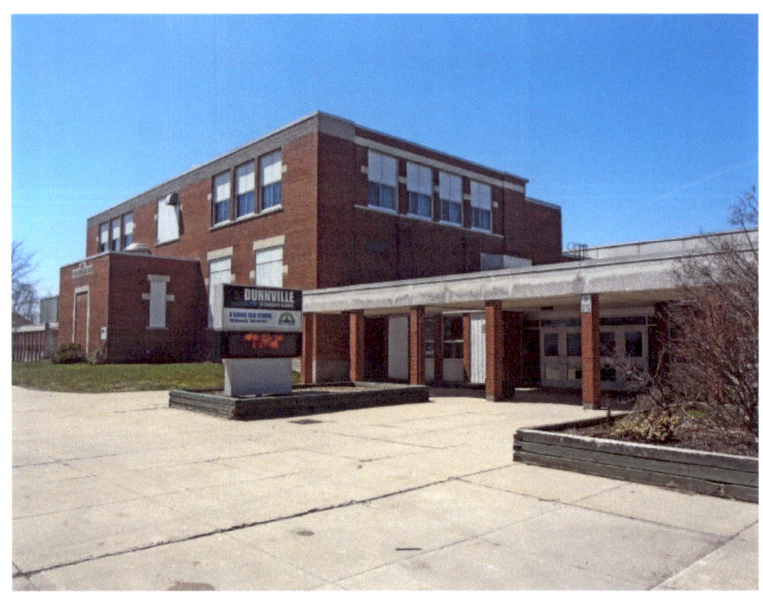

110 Helena Street (corner of Cedar Street) – Dunnville Secondary School - 1911

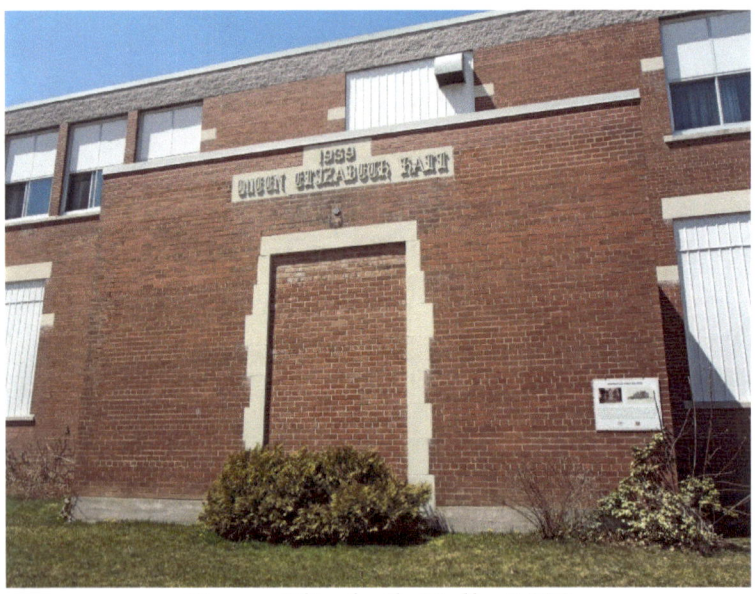

Queen Elizabeth Hall – 1939

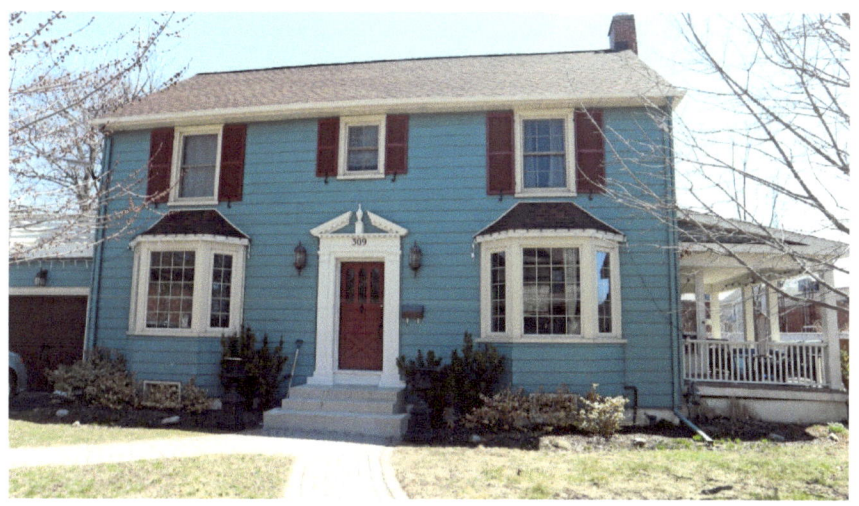

309 Cedar Street – broken pediment above entrance

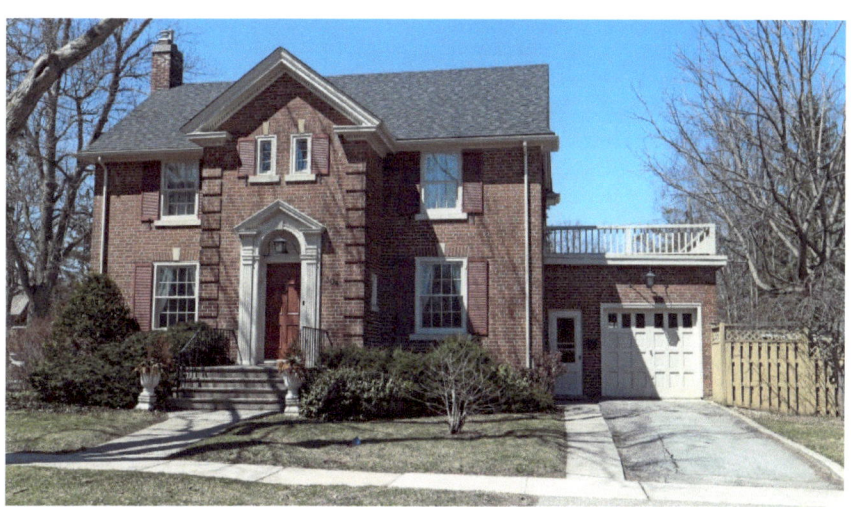

304 Church Street – two-storey frontispiece with quoins and cornice return on gable

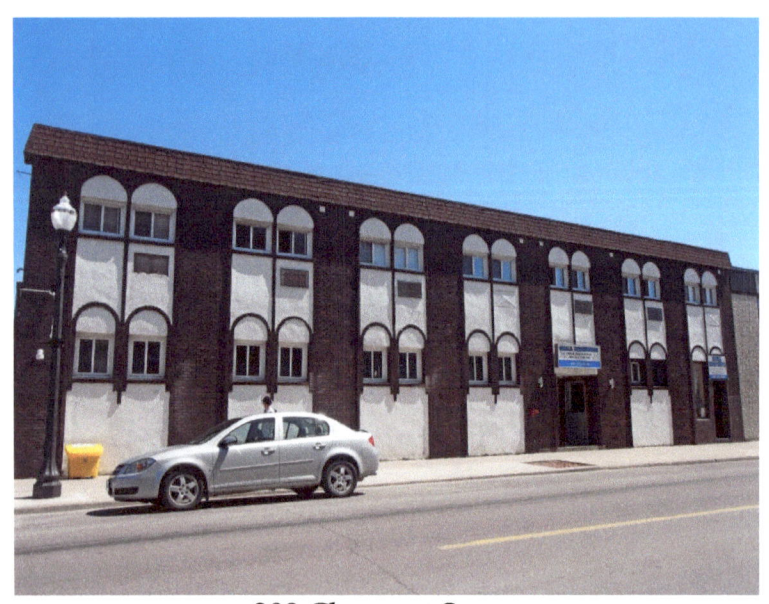

209 Chestnut Street

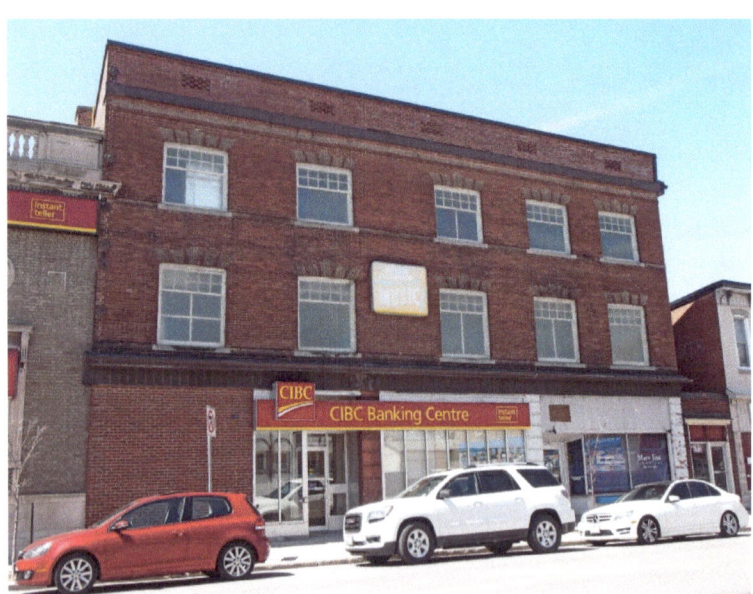

210 Chestnut Street

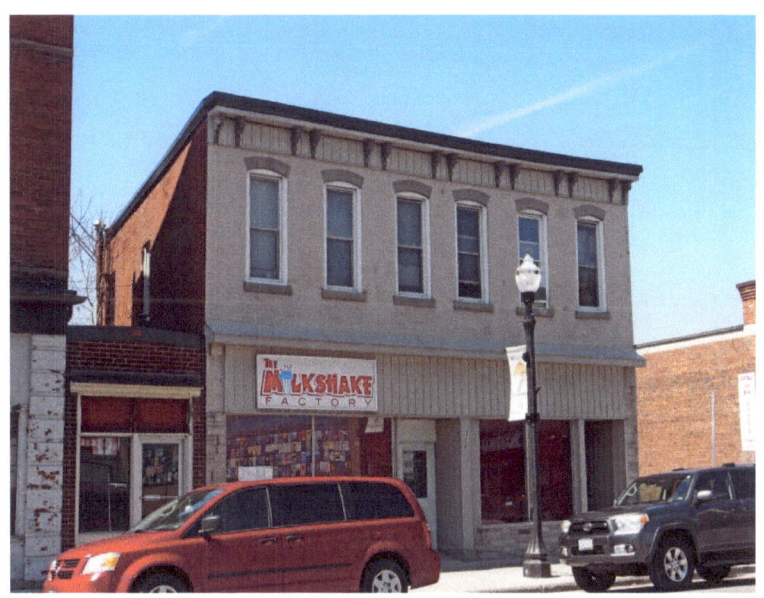

214 Chestnut Street

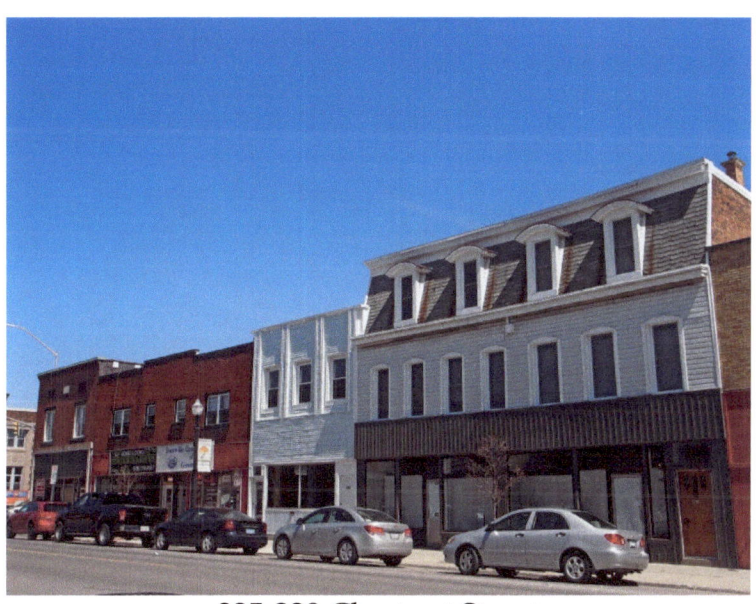

225-229 Chestnut Street

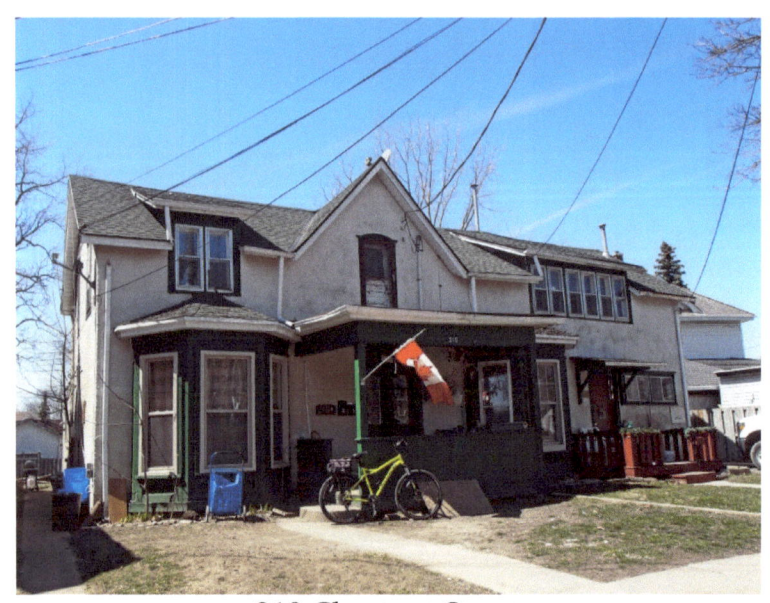

310 Chestnut Street

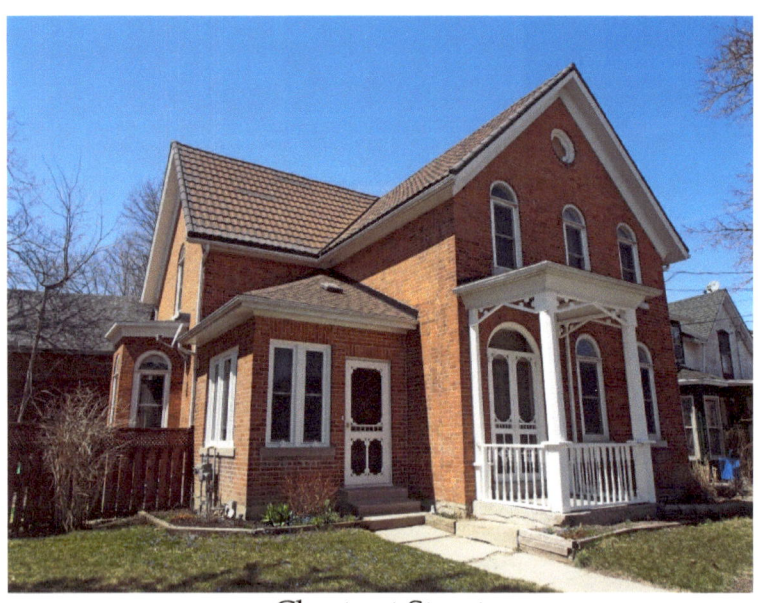

Chestnut Street

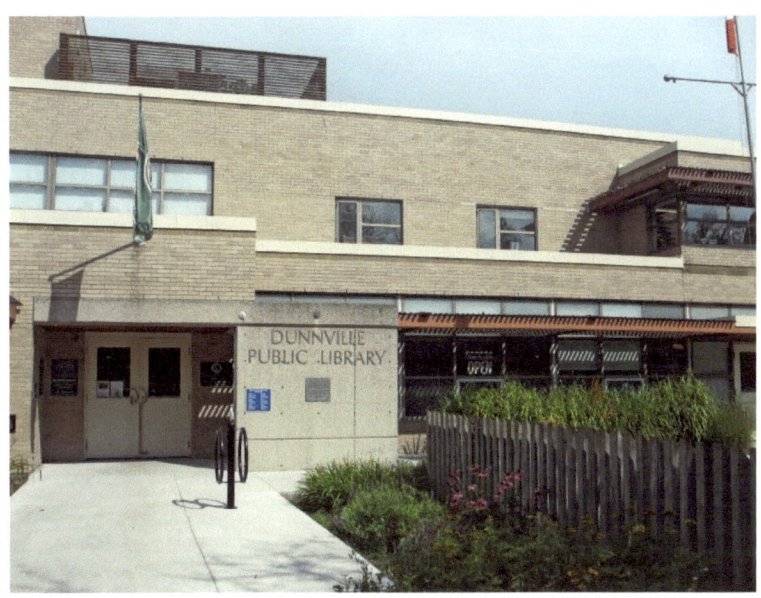

317 Chestnut Street – Dunnville Public Library

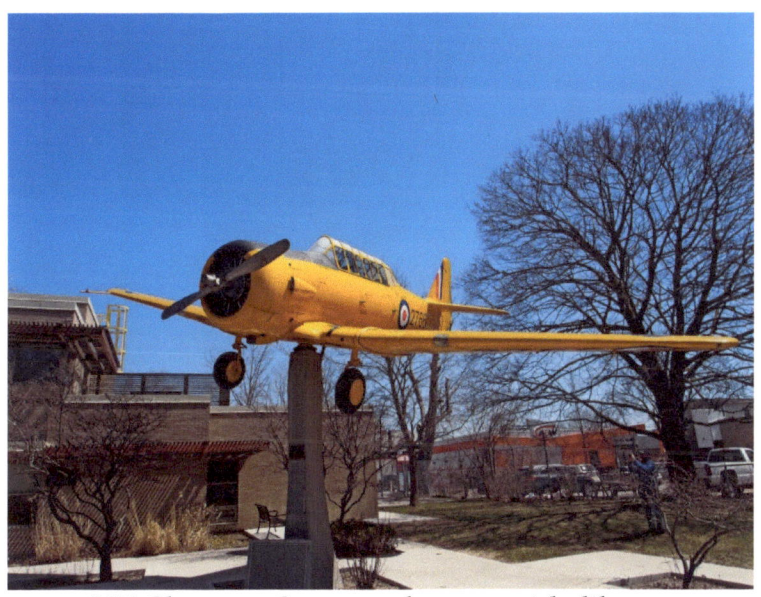

317 Chestnut Street – plane outside library

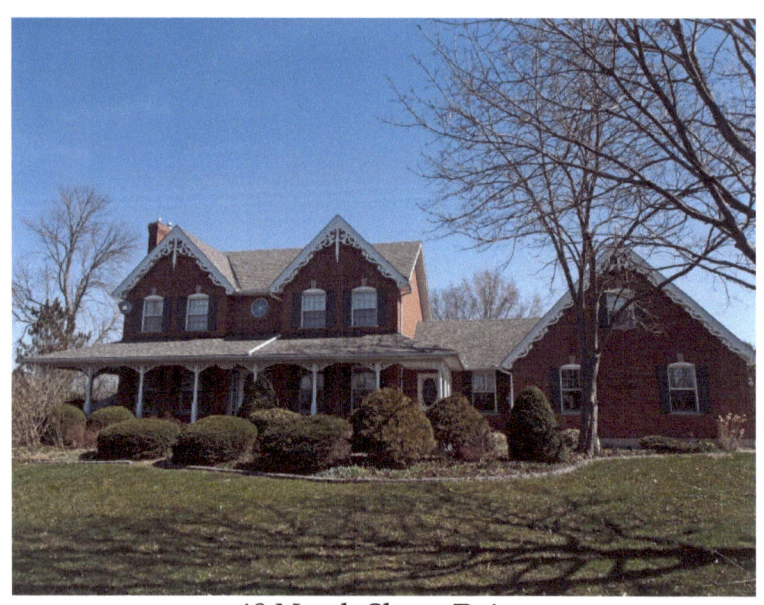

48 North Shore Drive

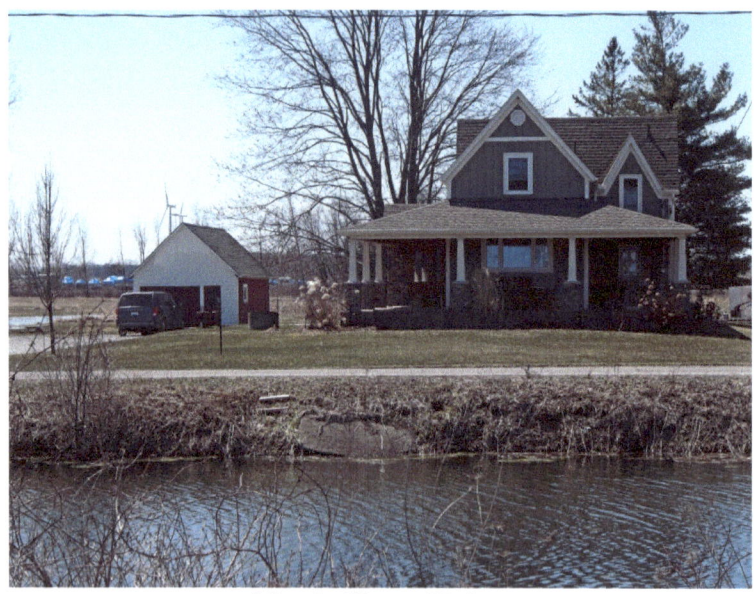

North Shore Drive

Building Styles

Beaux Arts: Promoters of this style sought to express the classical principles on a grand and imposing scale. Many of the Beaux Arts buildings were banks, post offices, and railway stations. The Ontario Beaux Arts style is eclectic mixing elements of Classical, Renaissance and Baroque. Often the designs have a temple-like façade, porticos with pediments, balustrades, and capitals in many styles.

Edwardian, 1900-1930 – This style bridges the ornate and elaborate styles of the Victorian era and the simplified styles of the 20th century. Edwardian Classicism provided simple, balanced facades, simple rooflines, dormer windows, large front porches, and smooth brick surfaces. Voussoirs and keystones are used sparingly and are understated. Finials and cresting are absent. Cornice brackets and braces are block-like and openings have flat arches or plain stone lintels.

Georgian, before 1860 – This style began with the British King Georges in the 18th century. These buildings have balanced facades around a central door, medium-pitched gable roofs, and small paned windows.

Gothic Revival, 1830-1890 – These decorative buildings have sharply-pitched gables with highly detailed verge boards, pointed-arch window openings, and dichromatic brickwork. It is a common style in Ontario.

Italianate, 1850-1900 – A two story rectangular building with a mild hip roof, a projecting frontispiece, and generous eaves with ornate cornice brackets was the basis of the style; often there are large sash windows, quoins, ornate detailing on the windows, belvederes and wraparound verandahs. Italianate commercial buildings often have cast iron cresting and elegant window surrounds.

Neo-Colonial (also Colonial Revival, Georgian Revival or Neo-Georgian) architecture seeks to revive elements of architectural style of American colonial architecture of the period around the Revolutionary War which drew strongly from Georgian architecture of Great Britain. Architecture from the 18th and early 19th centuries in Ontario includes a wide assortment of detailing and ornament applied to a design centered around the fireplace and the source of water. Structures are typically two stories, have a symmetrical front facade with elaborate front doorways, often with decorative crown pediments, fanlights, and sidelights, symmetrical windows flanking the front entrance, often in pairs or threes, and columned porches.

Romanesque Revival, 1880-1910 – This style hearkens back to medieval architecture of the 11th and 12th centuries with a heavy appearance, blocky towers and rounded arches.

Saltbox: A saltbox is a building with a long, pitched roof that slopes down to the back, generally a wooden frame house. A saltbox has just one storey in the back and two stories in the front. The asymmetry of the unequal sides and the long, low rear roof line are the most distinctive features of a saltbox, which takes its name from its resemblance to a wooden lidded box in which salt was once kept. The earliest saltbox houses were created when a lean-to addition was added onto the rear of the original house extending the roof line sometimes to less than six feet from ground level.

Tudor Revival – exposed timbers with stucco infill, multi-paned windows.

Vernacular/Traditional Mode 1638 - 1950
Influenced but not defined by a particular style, vernacular buildings are made from easily available materials and exhibit local design characteristics.

Other Books by Barbara Raue

Coins of Gold
Arrows, Indians and Love
The Life and Times of Barbara
The Cromwell Family Book
Laura Secord Discovered
Daddy Where Are You?

Montana Series
Book 1: Montana Dream
Book 2: Life on the Montana Frontier
Book 3: Montana to Boston and Back
Book 4: Montana Sons Go to War
Book 5: Montana Sons Return from War

Visit Barbara's website to view all of her books
http://barbararaue.ca

Other books on Haldimand County:
Fisherville, Nanticoke and Selkirk Ontario in Colour Photos
Cayuga and York Ontario in Colour Photos
Dunnville Ontario Book 2 and Other Haldimand County towns in Colour Photos
Hagersville Ontario in Colour Photos
Jarvis and Port Dover Ontario in Colour Photos

Barbara is The Authority on Saving Our History One Photo at a Time. She is pursuing her interest in photography and architecture by preserving a record through photos of old buildings from the 1800s and 1900s with their unique architecture. Enjoy the beautiful architecture in the comfort of your living room. Dream about what it was like in those by-gone days. Dream about what it was like to live in a mansion like one of those in this book.

Barbara Raue, a wife, mother and grandmother, is an avid reader and writer. She has researched and compiled several family histories. In 2010, Barbara published her book "Coins of Gold," which celebrates the courageous life of her mother, May Todd. Barbara's second book is a historical fiction "Arrows, Indians and Love" which takes place in Boonesborough, Kentucky during the time of Daniel Boone. In 2013, Barbara published *The Cromwell Family Book* in which she traces her ancestry generations back into Great Britain. Her second novel is called *Laura Secord Discovered,* in which the story of Laura's service during the War of 1812 is shared. Barbara's memoir is titled *Daddy Where Are You?* It tells of her life growing up without a father. Five novels in the Montana Series have been published, *Montana Dream, Life on the Montana Frontier, Montana to Boston and Back, Montana Sons Go to War*, and *Montana Sons Return from War*. The Donaldson series of two novels is available: *Rite of Passage* and *Rite of Marriage*.

This is a link to Barbara's website to view all of her books
http://barbararaue.ca

www.ingramcontent.com/pod-product-compliance
Lightning Source LLC
Chambersburg PA
CBHW041941240526
45473CB00033B/184